NOW THAT WE HAVE TO

WALK

NOW THAT WE HAVE TO
WALK

Exploring the Out-of-Doors

By

RAYMOND TIFFT FULLER

Essay Index Reprint Series

Originally Published by
E. P. DUTTON & CO., INC.
NEW YORK

BOOKS FOR LIBRARIES PRESS
FREEPORT, NEW YORK

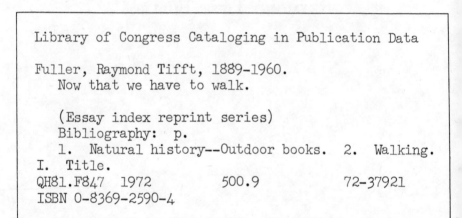

Library of Congress Cataloging in Publication Data

Fuller, Raymond Tifft, 1889-1960.
  Now that we have to walk.

  (Essay index reprint series)
  Bibliography: p.
  1. Natural history--Outdoor books. 2. Walking.
I. Title.
QH81.F847 1972   500.9   72-37921
ISBN 0-8369-2590-4

PRINTED IN THE UNITED STATES OF AMERICA
BY
NEW WORLD BOOK MANUFACTURING CO., INC.
HALLANDALE, FLORIDA 33009

The most precious things of life are near at hand, without money and without price. Each of you has the whole wealth of the universe at your very doors. All that I ever had, and still have, may be yours by stretching forth your hand and taking it.

—JOHN BURROUGHS

TABLE OF CONTENTS

ACKNOWLEDGMENTS

The author and publisher are grateful for permission to reprint herein from the published works of others, as follows:

Edwin Tenney Brewster, from *This Puzzling Planet* (The Bobbs-Merrill Company)

John Burroughs, from *John Burroughs' Works* (Houghton Mifflin Company)

Lansing Christman, "Hills Like These" (*The Washington Post*)

William W. Christman, from *The Untillable Hills* and *Songs of the Western Gateway* (courtesy of Mrs. William W. Christman)

Alan Devoe, from *The Over-Civilized* (Coward McCann, Inc.)

Raymond L. Ditmars, from *Westchester Countryside* Magazine (courtesy of Miss Gladys Ditmars)

Glenn Ward Dresbach, "Wild Goose Feather" (*The New York Times*)

Wainwright Evans, from "Mother of a Million" (*Better Homes and Gardens*)

Fred Lape, "Strawberry Picker" (*The New York Times*)

Maurice Maeterlinck, from *The Life of the Bee* (Dodd, Mead and Company, Inc.)

Daniel Smythe, "On Turning Over a Stone" (*The Washington Post*)

Louis Stoddard, "Miracles and Nothing More" (*The New York Times*)

Portions of the author's text have appeared in several periodicals. He thanks the following magazines for extending their permission to republish excerpts in the present book from "Out Into All Outdoors" (*Delineator*, Hearst Magazines, Inc.), "Nature's Night Club" (*This Week*), "In Winter" (*Travel*), "On April Mornings" (*The Parents' Magazine*), "The New American Wilderness" (*The Saturday Evening Post*), and the poems, "Introductions" (formerly "My World," *Christian Science Monitor*) and "Winter Cordwood" (*Yankee*).

Thanks are also due The John Day Company for permission to reprint the chapter entitled "Knee-Deep In Marsh," taken from the volume, *Walk, Look and Listen!* by Raymond Tifft Fuller.

NOW THAT WE HAVE TO
WALK

Testimony After Conversion

This night under the evening star,
in the dimming sunset,
from the midst of my new acres,
I who have fled the phantom of cities
dedicate myself to the earth!
With dew soaked feet I stand
in the furrow of my cleaving,
in the rows of my planting;
the mantle of the earth has fallen upon me.

Escaped bondsman, I return to the soil:
here in evening's full ritual I pledge myself
seven times seven years to indenture —
I pledge *my life!*

I dedicate myself to the earth,
for I am the peasant of all lands, of all ages;
from my soil-lust emerges all cities.
Dumbly, doggedly I shall die
protecting these acres I have wrested,
spoils of my lone battle with destiny.
— Let others be shepherds of men,
binders of wounds, husbanders of kine,
fishers in the sea, hewers of wood;
but I shall garden this small earth and till it.
Henceforth my fealty is not to man,
nor to charity, science, letters, machines —
my dedication is to the earth!

Earth, I will tilt thy veiled chin
and smile into thy omnipotent eyes,
knowing not fear nor the import of fear! —
My feet are upon the ground.

CHAPTER I

TO BEGIN WITH

BERNARD SHAW is right of course when he states that a book's foreword is the part always written last. As I sit down to finish rereading this book's manuscript before bidding it good-by, I am penning a sort of farewell preface.

The conclusion forces itself upon me that by this date probably everything that could be written has been written about nature, about life in the country, its joys and satisfactions; the coming of Spring, the going of Fall; the delights of loafing, the humbling effects of bee-keeping, the scents of azalea, grape and locust, the exciting contacts with wild life, etc. Much writing, and varied. Most of it sincere, worthy; a large amount of it distinguished; some of it classic. — Signed by such names as Darwin, Fabre, Forel, Muir, Burroughs, Audubon, Hudson, Thoreau; not to mention the Mediterranean ancients and the nature poets, quick and dead, who have graced our tongue's literature. In the intellectual company of these, and more recently of such observers as Hornaday, Roosevelt, Torrey, 'Grayson', Seton-Thompson, Grinnell, Forbush, Hingston, Sanderson, Beebe, Eaton, Peattie, Long, Ditmars, Sharp, Chapman, Devoe, Olive Miller and *many* others, an American of today cannot possibly be allowed to assert that familiarity with and meticulous attention to the trivia of nature is merely fad, hobby or pastime. For these are not the names of dilettantes or entertainers; their literature is not apologia for a "flight from the city" or for an "escape from reality." They all have hold on something eternal and fundamental. What they have added to literature, to their own pleasure and to the world's, is weighty testimony of the mature, rich cultural

[13]

elements to be garnered from nature lore and the outdoor life.

Just now how we need that maturity and that culture! — The ability to face facts however grim! Humanity has got itself tied up in a kind of social and economic cat's cradle so intricate, so tangled that we are unable to find either end or beginning to the skein. But this, I think, is true: that the snarl has not its causes in nature; no, not in the vital biologic nature-of-man.

The red rule of tooth and claw is less harsh in fact than in seeming. There is a balance in undisturbed nature between food and feeder, hunter and prey, so that the resources of the earth are never idle. Some plants or animals may seem to dominate the rest, but they do so only so long as the general balance is maintained. The whole world of living things exists as a series of communities, whose order and permanence put to shame all but the most successful of human enterprise.[1]

The present warring state of the world of mankind; its deliberate cruelties and unprimate viciousness; somehow seems to be a perversion of that novel, strange thing the Mind; rather than a product of the truly biological character of *homo sapiens* on whom evolution has been laboring so long. — Perhaps clearer to say that animal-man's unique tool of offense and defense, his brain, seems to have failed signally in his transition from the hunter-planter stages into a more social level of existence. It is candid to state that no wild animal *hates* another, though there are numberless parasitisms, the preying of one species upon another

[1] From *Deserts On The March*, by Paul B. Sears. (Univ. of Okla. Press, 1935) — One of the notable books of its decade; recommended to every reader of this book.

for existence. No emotion in such processes, however, corresponds to hate; to calculating, egoistic destruction "for the good of the stronger species." Nowhere does nature's ecology hold place for a master race, a species which must survive though all others perish. Nature holds no distinctions of rank or birth to emphasize by display or maintain through cruelty; she has no need of pomp and magnificence. Nature is as regardful of moss as man; of a lichen as of a redwood. The State of Nature has no slums; in no species is there a "submerged tenth"; nor is one-third of a species ill-fed. The glen is as full of marvel as the hillside, and as pregnant with future life. And the sea is as fertile as the land. In the leaf a certain grandeur circulates; on the Himalayas is grandeur too. And it is Man alone who slays for hate and for glory instead of for life.

✻   ✻   ✻

This book will be listed as another Nature Book. What — another! . . . Again and again in the past after I have set down a few words about an experience which has stirred or delighted me; some sudden glimpse over the edge of Infinity, or the hearing or reading of certain "words which are windows to eternal things"; within a few weeks I find in a book something which reveals that I am (at fifty) merely a youth-growing-up; my predecessors, my elders, even my contemporaries appear to have noted it before. There is practically no spot on earth where a human foot has not stood. . . . Then why more? Why do successions of us nature-writers continue to turn out volumes which in a sense are repetitive and redundant? — Merely as evidence of a perennial urge toward self-expression? the flaunting of a type of literary competence? No, these are not the reasons we publish and publish after we write and write; it is due to a sort of persistent ecclesiasticism deep within so many

[15]

individuals. To propagandize the faith, our faith. Having
discovered a sort of salvation, or assurance in the heart of
nature; in the true, the beautiful, the vital elements of the
pulsating world we live in; a kind of nepenthe in walking,
looking, listening, studying; having found so much for
ourselves, we, like Calvin, "cannot choose but exhort."

And what we are doing, it seems to me after mature
reflection, turns out to be trying to maintain the morale
of all those who resist and oppose America's over-powering
cult of materialism and its high esteem of wealth, towards
which we are inherently conscientious objectors. — A
strange obsession? or an admirable defense? In all walks
of life a surprising number of people will be met who are
such evangelists at heart, though their various credos may
derive from no current religious or political platform. From
such comes this ever-widening volume of nature literature.

This protest, plus the actual abandonment of big cities
in late years, evidences, I think, a growing revulsion against
servitude to machinery and possessions; betokens an
"escape" in the best intent of the word; an increasing migration from a too severe, too unsatisfying existence. A migration full of meaning, which may presently be recognized
as an urge to create a new environment, one more fitting
for modernized man to exist in, now that he has a world
full of latent, unexploited power and is heir to all the tools
and the knowledge of his ancestry. . . . I have such a hope. —
After hate has at last burned itself out, and we become
natural and animal-like!

❄   ❄   ❄

Over a decade ago Walter Pritchard Eaton set down a
wise footnote to life:

"To rediscover the world of simplicities, the joy of creating with one's hands, the profound satisfactions of express-

ing an inner sense of beauty through the manipulation of visible forms — trees, plants, notes of music, or what not — the relief from a slackened quest for Things, is to discover, perhaps, one's self."

—There is no "perhaps" about it, Mr. Eaton. . . .

With pail in hand she walks the field.
Her dresses plow the nodding clover.
Her eyes watch for the red concealed
under the grass when it bends over.
Seventy-two, and berrying still.
It was always so when she was young.
She had a gypsy love of a hill
whenever berries were ripe among
its knee-deep grass; there she was free;
the day was hers to look and roam,
to lunch in the shade beneath a tree
and feel the earth and the sky her home.

The sun and wind go over the grass.
The bobolink sings, and the meadowlark.
The years come back, the old years pass
like shadows moving out of the dark;
they come and are gone; she sighs and feels
them slip from her like clothes at night
until she is young again. She kneels
and picks; her face is filled with light.

—FRED LAPE

CHAPTER II

NOW THAT WE HAVE TO WALK

WE who lived through the last war have seen remarkable shifts in mores and manners — no need to list them here. Then we passed through our country's worst depression and witnessed a few other unforeseeable changes come into our lives. The Greater World War is on; we will have more changes. Most of us are in divers ways working harder and longer, if not fighting or being prepared to fight. Leisure already is a more sober and appreciated thing. The automobile has been retired for a while from the front lines to rest-billets. I have a feeling that even if it comes back soon, to a certain degree the heart will have gone out of motoring, just motoring. — In greater degree if we (some of us) have meantime walked far enough away from the family car to look back and see it steadily and see it whole: the car as symbol for an Order of Things, a way of living which we considered (if we gave it a thought) as fixed and ultimate.

About now we are (some of us) trying perforce to find our relaxations in interests and recreations new to us; activities simpler and cheaper; less cluttered by gear, garb and grounds than those with which we grew up. We are not only in a worried-but-confident state about the war's outcome and the ultimate adjustments all may have to make; we are somewhat humbled, somewhat ashamed of our breathless races with the Joneses. In place of touring, of week-end housefuls, of pretentious and far away vacations, we may be obliged to substitute days afoot, odd hours closer to a book, — or to the heart of Nature, the

ultimate soother and sphinx. And that in the end may prove
to have been altogether a good thing.

Probably for the same "reason" that a dismaying proportion of us Americans buy too many superfluous gadgets to
save time and labor (working still harder than ever to
possess and maintain them); neglect our health and our
insurance, and live always a little above our income-level;
we have put far too much of our "saved" time into being
entertained. Seductively placed before us is a variety of
more or less effete diversions perhaps never equalled since
the days of the Caesars. Eighteenth century royalties never
had the time-killing opportunities we common Americans
have. We are being painstakingly trained to regard entertainment and ever more entertainment as the crowning
feature of civilized life. Subtly the passive role has been
glorified into being the characteristic element of a high
standard of living. Being entertained has come to preoccupy
life on an international scale, and entertainment is a huge
vested interest eager to perpetuate itself. Millions of Americans have surrendered all personal sovereignty over their
fun and their interests. Patent it is that they who fatten
bank accounts thereby, largely determine what, where and
alongside whom we shall eat, drink and be merry; how and
wherewith we shall be clothed. They establish the Correct
Thing as authoritatively as a Headman of the Hottentots
lays his tabus. And now, more deftly than ever, an inherent
anthropoid suggestibility, congenital with *Homo sapiens,*
is being exploited — almost within sound of the guns! —
"Money for bonds," yes, but money for buncombe first.

Hired copy-writers, illustrators and radio voices have for
years been persuading us that passing time, languidly,
expensively is the ideal way for American thoroughbreds
to put in their spare hours; everywhere spreads the tip
(from Shakespeare) "that the hand of little employment

hath the daintier sense." Quite as the Puritans were drilled
to regard the world as a mere tarrying place on the brief
journey to Heaven which is our home, so the counterpart
idea has been and is being inserted into our Unconscious:
that it matters little what we put into our days if only we
accept them as offered us, ready-made, stylized; that to file
the days behind us as consumers and payers rather than
as participators, is the pattern of honest citizenship. Killing
time in approved tailor-made ways is held to be the hall-
mark of culture. So adroitly assured that the filled life is
equivalent to the full life, most of us have come fully to
believe it.

At length we (some of us) have wondered just why we
do not get a lot of happiness out of eternally being entertained. For in the end passive pleasures do not satisfy.
Like a cake and ice cream diet, we cannot live on them.
And we suddenly see that all those sit-down-and-admire
avocations, those activities performed by others and "enjoyed" by us as observers, are truly second-hand living. And
a bit of it goes a long way. Second-hand living is, biologically considered at least, no way to live at all. Our muscles
must work and our glands sweat or shortly we suffer. Yet
biologic aspects are on only one side of the passive-ist's
coin; for, as we everywhere observe, being entertained, like
a drug addiction, calls always for the slavery of larger and
larger doses. And too, the fan-and-fanny type of life is such
a quicksand that one just cannot get across it anywhere.
— For youngsters the pathetic habit is probably worst; trying to erect a life, a personality, a character around sheer
entertainment has been perhaps what is chiefly "the matter
with" the younger set — if anything is. Surely, no people
widely infected by passive-ism ever conquered a continent
from sea to sea, or won a two-ocean war!

Who would deny — and I haven't — that relaxation is

NOW THAT WE HAVE TO WALK

necessary. Many of us absolutely need it; if only to shut out
the war horrors for a few hours a week. — Yet, why not
constructive relaxation? — Constructive relaxation — shades
of long Winter evenings and Summer's war-saving time!
With modern America as full of a number of things as the
trains between New York and Washington — why should
we lack choice, our own choice? Why not such things as
wood carving, weaving, carpentry, linoleum blocking, etching, theatricals, plaster modelling, gardening, sketching,
photography . . . most especially, *why not try Nature?* Why
not Walking; walking *as a fine art*. Nature flowers best and
fullest through Walking. It is the open sesame to all outdoors. . . . You will promptly discover that handbooks on
this and that avocation, indoor or out, so crowd library
shelves that you could almost pick them out blindfolded.
So, after all, what the baffled biped requires is only a self-
starter.

*   *   *

Whenever these front porch, fireside and dinner table
discussions get started appertaining to "What shall we
Americans do with the *New* Leisure; what will our children
do after the war? — *without a car even?* How can we get
anywhere or do anything"— we nature hobbyists only sit
back quietly and listen. We smile, probably in a superior,
self-satisfied way which must be infuriatingly tactless. For
we believe that worry about the ever-growing shortening
of labor hours, about an impending mass production of
leisure in the next generation, is needless. We are sorry for
our friends who have grasped no concept of leisure save
being entertained; those who know the *at-loss* feeling most
acutely. But we do know the answer about gluts in the
leisure market — *there isn't any*. There won't be. I mean,
there needn't be any surplus. We are confident that no

[22]

NOW THAT WE HAVE TO WALK

matter at what new low leisure preferred is to be quoted,
a nature lover always will know how to absorb unlimited
shares of it.

But to get that answer across! How to make our harried
friends see it as we see it is difficult. I know, because at first
I used patiently to try telling them about it — Plain enough
to me. Not only in theory but in practice. Had I not been
burning up leisure for over thirty years; burning it at both
ends of the day, the week, the year? And asking for more?
Rarely finding anywhere near enough bye-time. Finding
June days even not long enough. Actually grudging sleep
its seven or eight unconscious hours. A glutton for entertainment — self-entertainment.—The days fled on; here it
was May, credit it or not; in a few moments it was June;
before one realized, came November.— All in spite of my
grasping at every day, too.— Like Poe, though not quite so
desperately:

> "I hold within my hand
> Grains of the golden sand —
> How few! yet how they creep
> Through my fingers to the deep,
> While I weep — while I weep!
> O God! can I not grasp
> One with a tighter clasp?
> O God! can I not save
> *One* from the pitiless wave? . . ."

Grains of the golden sand of life: days of walking, watching, discovering, admiring, thinking, enjoying! Alas, the
sands of that beach *are* numbered!

A *leisure-problem*, forsooth! We outdoor fanatics for
years had been crowding and crowding workaday hours
to the wall; pilfering half-hours here and hours there; com-
mitting frequent grand larcenies of whole week-ends: our

salary checks in constant jeopardy. In consequence scandalizing our higher salaried brethren. We never got enough. Beggars of life. Thieves of existence. . . .

And now, it appears, just ahead of us all, if we are winning the peace, are to be shorter job-days and job-weeks. And you (some of you) are asking, "What shall we do — what shall our children do — with all the new labor-saving devices we can buy; when everything is cheap and work is short? — How shall we educate for The New Leisure?" — *Well, I give up!*

No! No, I'll not give it up yet! One more go at it, presenting the all too obvious solution. . . . This is it; these paragraphs may be my swan-song. Yet should I expect too quick a persuasion; after all? Perhaps the way is to be evolution not revolution. Is it not education which is modernly accepted, at least by intellectuals, to be the only *true* reforming principle in this somewhat democratic America? — Keeping patiently at it; starting with the children; continuing by adult education, etc.? . . .

Here is a succinct six-point program — I almost wrote *prescription*. To offer it is the reason this book is written.

1. *Determine* to take up Walking, Bicycling and a Nature Hobby. *One* at the outset; others if need arises will develop later. — At the beginning it is imperative to *want to.* — First the psychic self-starter.

2. Buy one, two or three handbooks pertaining to your selected hobby; make the local museum and/or library an additional authoritative reference-book on the subject. Don't be book-shy, be shelf-conscious!

3. Force yourself to get out of doors as often as possible. (And I don't want to know how you get there!) Choose at least one ample rambling-range, explore it, learn it.

NOW THAT WE HAVE TO WALK

(A half an hour is better than a loaf elsewhere.) And always wear your oldest, most worn-out clothes and shoes — and like them!

4. Attach to yourself a similarly equipped companion. *Not two or more* — unless they be those children of yours. (—Incidentally, one of the most blessed "breaks" which can befall you is to have married a *companion*.)

5. Patiently acquire background; i. e. build up a modest list of the things you first recognize and feel at home with; so that from this terra firma you can mount on stepping stones to rarer things. (Sketching such specimens is an effective, if prosaic practice; an aid to memory, affording the data for that "process of elimination" upon which is founded everyone's identifying skill. One lady of my acquaintance mastered over 200 plant identifications in two seasons by this journeyman method; and passed from tyro to expert.)

6. *Keep at it until you can't stop.*

*   *   *

"For to admire an' for to see,
For to be'old this world so wide —
It never done no good to me,
But I can't drop it if I tried!"

Yet, possibly, it may do *you* some good.— So much to see, so much of marvel and surprise; so much to do; so many places to go! . . . No matter what line one's nature enthusiasms take, by and large it can be asserted that "the more miles, the more joys."— You see, above all, that self-participation is the keynote sounding beneath my fugue. Boredom

[25]

NOW THAT WE HAVE TO WALK
(like acid stomach) inevitably arises from being entertained too much; self-entertainment can never be boring.—
Just here is where we will kill or cure Leisure! Living can
never become unbearable if it is unborable.

CHAPTER III

THE NEW AMERICAN WILDERNESS

Many reasons have been adduced for the unrest and imbalance currently upsetting the world. . . Hardly anyone appears to have suggested the most obvious of all possible reasons — that the trouble with civilization is simply the fact that it is too civilized. . . .

The resolute effort of our civilization has been toward destroying as thoroughly as possible the ancient natural bonds which once bound us to our earth. By a thousand ingenious inventions we have insured that Civilized Man need never again know the feel of rain against his skin, never need break and sift the soil with his hands. . . . By myriad devices we have labored to cut off those racial tap-roots which originally were deep thrusted in the earth. . .

The old rhythms of living have been abolished. . . he *is* as remote from the rituals of earth as tho he were no creature of it at all. . . .

Once upon a time it was a man's consuming ambition to own a piece of land which he could till and cultivate and make the site of his home. When he took title to his plot of soil he acquired a great deal more than a piece of real estate. He came into possession of a sense of security and inward peace. His universe now had a point of focus, and from his stewardship over soil and plant and tree he learned the meaning of responsibility. . . . We have changed all that. . . .

—ALAN DEVOE: *Down to Earth*

THE NEW AMERICAN WILDERNESS

A CHICKEN in every pot, at every backdoor a two-car garage and two cars in each. . . . All at once a miracle happened. A cataclysm not unlike that which created the crumpled Alleghenies at the end of Ordovician time! Really and truly, as in a dream, the Gasoline Age faltered, wobbled, missed, slowed down, all but stopped! It was as if Rip Van Winkle had waked, to see — to stare at the broad Hudson Valley suddenly repeopled by dinosaurs or herds of eohippi. Who could have imagined that! . . .

✿   ✿   ✿

The writer has been wondering of late if a great many people, particularly those over forty, did not heave smothered sighs of relief when the car was laid up.— Along with its bills: oil, gasoline, insurance, repairs . . . and you know what else.— Along with the noise, odor, jam, death-rate; from, of course, *other-people's*-cars. Myself am not so tottering old, yet I am bound to regard the automobile as an innovation; and do, in surreptitious moments, feel twinges of distrust and skepticism about its indispensableness. . . .

A legendary "little boy in school" once wrote that "pins has saved hundreds of lives — by people not swallering them." War, rubber starvation and submarine blockade may possibly save hundreds of miles and hours of health, zest and new interests, simply by "people not using them"— *autos*, I mean. Not merely because a new dignity is discovered for human feet but also because a larger spiritual investment is being made in leisure time. Many of us never before seemed to grasp what a relatively important fraction of our lifetime was being spent simply as chauffeurs; non-professionally, of course; but nevertheless occupied merely as machine-tenders whose attention must constantly be focused on the mechanics of operating it, while most of the world was a blur both optically and mentally.

Yet one simply may not say that "maybe the loss of the car is a blessing in disguise," or "America got along all right without the auto thirty years ago, it can now."— No, the mode of life and work is now so altered by its universal use that to be deprived of cars now is a serious national hardship.

Yet not a hardship only, because a sizeable sector of living in, on, and around motoring was softship and little else.

Do you recall the tides of contrition and humility that set in during the years 1930-35? Practically everyone, looking backward at the foolishness, extravagances and puerile economic assumptions of the Twenties, began parroting: "Why, we oughta *known* that couldn't last! It was a pipe-dream, a joy-ride. . . ."

Well, the pipe may have gone out temporarily, but what transpired shortly was that the joy-riding came back in altered form; the joy part of it mostly residing in the effort-lessness and pride with which we employed gasoline-burning as a virtually complete substitute for both mortgage-burning and muscular activity. As a people, we invested during some twenty years incalculable billions not only in the cars but in roads, bridges, garages, filling stations, traffic police, petroleum, tankers, advertising, etc., etc. A major part of this investment was of course for pleasure-car operation. Did we get it back; are we getting it back in the "health, pleasure, relaxation and high standards of life" which universal motoring was supposed to exude? — Not at least by 1936 when Mr. Roosevelt first

[29]

NOW THAT WE HAVE TO WALK .
told about "one-third of a nation . . ." — you can finish the
quotation. (Nor by 1940, when he reiterated it.) — Not if,
on a basis of its costing a car owner from $300 to $400
annually (and directly) to be an owner; much of which,
soberly pondered, should have been spent for housing,
nutrition, dental, medical and hospital care, for hobbies and
relaxations, for books and other cultural and educational
ends. That $300 to $400 is approximately *half the average
annual family income* in the United States!

Paying that huge bill for "the Motor Age" was probably
the main cause of the rapid centralizing (or federalizing)
of political and economic power during the '30s. Inasmuch
as the bill could not be met out of the incomes of the great
majority of car owners; and at the same time allow these
owners to meet their own share of the cost of medical care,
dentistry, schooling, higher education and other charges
upon the good life; the local community at first tried to
contribute, as charity or relief, part of the cost; then had
to call upon the State; then the State had to call for federal
help. Whereupon bureaucracies and commissions and federal taxations sprouted and flourished like grass — never
to be cut down and to wither. Unemployment as a nation-
wide innovation may have been in part due to the same
fact: that so much family spending finally poured into
motoring and its allied lines, almost nothing was left in the
average family budget to keep very many other industries —
and agriculture — alive on the scale to which they had been
accustomed. So these did wither. In short, America had
been living beyond its means. No blinking the fact! . . .

✿   ✿   ✿

Meanwhile a wave of arteriosclerosis, circulatory ills, kid-
ney defaults and other so-called degenerative breakdowns,
[*30*]

began warning the life-insurance watch-dogs that flabby
bodies and flabbier eating, drinking and sleeping customs
were danger signals. And they began to bark loudly. By
1942 pretty much the whole pack of nutritionists, medical
men and draft-boards joined in the din. "We oughta known
that couldn't last" is again dawning upon us. The automo-
bile-as-culture plainly had let us down again. . . . What
plainly we *needed* was food and . . .[1]

Last July the head of the chemical engineering department of our largest university told a convention: "Industrial
developments arising from wartime researches may alter
the whole course of civilization here. Competent authorities
are convinced that the automobile industry has passed its
peak. It is believed that some of the largest producers
in the industry will not re-enter it." In 1941 who could have
imagined that!

At this point is high time for the appearance of my present
theme: moral substitutes for Motoring-as-an-end-in-itself.—
What of such truly ancient avocations as Walking, Bicycling, yes, and plain Reading; — reading not published books
solely, but the "books in the running brooks, sermons in
stones, and good (— or somehow good) in everything"?
We can no more "enjoy" nature from the motor-car than
from the Twentieth Century Limited; enjoy scenery or
landscape, perhaps, but not nature. It is a fixed law of the
universe that the path into nature must be followed on
foot. One may go on wheels to the start of the path but no
farther.

Has the automobiling age really "spoiled" the countryside, as so many honest city folk believe and assert? It has
not. Motoring is mainly two dimensional; or as the geome-
tries put it, "that which has direction only." Impressions as

[1] A 1942 FSA survey in seventeen states finds that "only four out of every
hundred persons in rural areas are in top-notch physical condition."

NOW THAT WE HAVE TO WALK
to wholesale overrunning and desecration have probably
gained common belief because of what motorist millions
have done to roadside spots and to public camping places.
Need I catalogue these atrocities? — But, if you have not
done so, go a little deeper in investigation; you may be
astonished at how slightly the out-of-doors has been disturbed. You can start, even from a big city, and in an hour's
run, or less, discover up a side road beautiful, disregarded
nooks, orchards, streams, woods, neglected pastures; all
with never a punctured beer can or a discarded ice cream
carton.— While perhaps a mile away creeps in The New
American Wilderness. . . . But let me reproduce part of an
article I wrote recently for a national magazine. It serves
as answer to the question at the beginning of this paragraph.

❖   ❖   ❖

Forty-five minutes from Broadway. That's where I lived
ten years ago; that's where I began to notice it ten years ago.
In the back yard of the most densely populated, most
extensive city area in America.— Even here the Wilderness
was coming back. . . . I have seen since that what was true
in the metropolitan district is also happening in scores of
suburban localities between Old Man River and the sunrise.
    That flashing beacon for aviators located on a skyscraper
top in mid-Manhattan — we could see its nervous beam of
light tirelessly sweeping across the night. The foghorns up
and down Long Island Sound crooned in the mist like
distant organ pipes. On a lowering evening the south-
western sky was rosy with reflections of New York's evening
bath of electricity. . . . Forty-five minutes from Broadway;
yet so different that we could have been as far as Singapore.
    The spot I refer to is bounded, east and west, by the two
great parkways that lead solid lines of motor traffic north-

ward out of the nation's largest city. I lived there for nine
years. If you had never explored that 600 acres of woodland
behind our home you would find it impossible to believe
that so much wild life could have endured so near to the
tremendous throb and pound of a great city. Twenty-five
miles from John D. Rockefeller's offices! Yet in early morning you would not have thought that the gasoline engine
had been invented. Beginning with evening twilight, you
would swear that Henry Ford was a myth.— More about
this particular paradise in a moment. First, I must do some
reporting about a striking change taking place, quietly,
relentlessly, extensively in the American countryside; a
renaissance of the wilderness of which the city public has
hardly been aware.

While it is true, as my own experience shows, that an
astonishing amount of animal and green life exists right
at our elbows, it is also true that east of the Mississippi, at
least, untended land is greatly increasing. There are numerous signs pointing to this conclusion. Paradoxical as it might
seem, what with our expanding population and the universal use of automobiles, many areas wherein the wearers
of furs, feathers and scales — the nonhuman ones, I mean —
were not long ago rated as rare or extinct, are seeing them
return again. The motor car has caused concrete roads to
shoot out in every direction and has diffused widening sub-
urbs roundabout every city. Yet a true wilderness, despite
gasoline, highways and vacations, slowly but surely edges
up to some of our city limits, nullifying much of the back-
breaking toil of our ancestors. Anyone traveling about the
country with an eye for such things is convinced that large
sectors are going back to a state of nature. That State and
Federal parks and preserves have increased steadily of late
is well-known. This magnificent realization of what conservation actually means to us and our descendants deserves

[33]

NOW THAT WE HAVE TO WALK

all praise. But when all these square miles are added up, these reservations are in extent almost negligible compared with the unplanned and unforeseen regression to Nature of farm lands which once were tamed.

Rural conditions in the East have all changed. The countryside is changing with them. Mr. Wheeler McMillen in his book *Too Many Farmers* makes the remarkable statement that between 1919 and 1927, as officially reported, 19,000,000 acres went out of cultivation and at least 76,000 farms ceased to exist as farms. During which period agricultural products increased twenty-five per cent. Farming has gone West. These statistics are several years old; the process has gone on steadily since then, as the recent census vividly proves. About a million acres annually continue to lapse. There were, and there still are, too many eastern farmers! — That is, *for their own good!*

In the rural district where I now reside — a district whose massive barns and large acreages, now going to decay, corroborate the local conviction as to its *once* superb fertility— eight large farms have been vainly on the market for years, deserted and surrendered wholly or in part to Nature's untiring persistence. There are no heirs who cared to work them and no buyers come to gamble on their luck as homesteaders. These pastures, meadows and once tilled fields are mostly uncared for. In their place is springing up the New Wilderness.

Go but a little way aside from the through highways of travel in a dozen Northeastern States, and you will find parallel conditions. Deserted farms are a drug on the market; farm values decrease annually. In addition, the workable acres of thousands of as yet undeserted farms are shrinking, their tenants either having recognized the imperative need of working less land, and that more intensively, or having despaired of even keeping their back lots

[34]

THE NEW AMERICAN WILDERNESS
and fence lines respectably subdued. Abundant help, large
families, are no more. — But Nature is as unwearying as
ever. Nature does not have depression-cycles, epidemics
and eras of hard times; she works ever at 100% capacity,
and dotes on overproduction. It is assuredly no joke to
keep a farm from being foreclosed by bushes and weeds,
as every farmer knows — to which knowledge I can add
my own mite of experience in trying to keep decent Sunday
clothes on thirty acres of my own!

That the skirmishes which have at last led to a major
victory for the Wilderness, actually began some seventy
years ago is not generally realized. Department of Agriculture records assert that in 1865 there was more cleared
land east of the Mississippi than there ever has been since!—
This, I submit, is one of the most significant facts which
those who are nibbling at farm problems, in Congress and
out, will ever have to face.

From a county clerk in New York's southern-tier, one
hunter in a recent Winter received cash for the scalps of
thirty-two bobcats. This is from one of the few counties
in the State nowadays paying a bounty on lynx; a so-called
agricultural county. I cannot recall the exact number of
weasels for which he told me he had also been paid bounty;
I believe it was over a hundred. He had likewise killed his
legal limit of black bears, deer and grouse, besides large
numbers of muskrats, raccoons and 'possums. Now that is
some hunting! Old inhabitants declare such a thing impossible twenty or thirty years ago. That particular county
has lost population since the beginning of the century.
Within rifle-shot of my home now in that general vicinity,
a splendid pasture, devoid of brush in 1920 and supplying
ample range for some forty head of cattle, now shelters
a small herd of deer the year around. I have seen twelve
of the lovely creatures at once, and have gazed incredu-

lously at the exact spot where a neighbor came upon twin
fawns last Spring. That pasture is now woods-and-thicket
combined. In October 1942, I have discovered that two
wild bears have taken residence within half a mile of my
house — a phenomenon which could not have occurred
here in something over a hundred years past.

On my many excursions in other sections of New York
and New England, especially in the Catskills, Green Mountains, northwestern Connecticut, and the Adirondack foothills, I have been watching the same increase of wilderness.
I should like to take you along a few of the all-but-over-
grown woods roads — which appear as highways on the
U. S. Geological Survey maps made in the '90s — covering
some of these areas. Farmhouse after farmhouse indicated
on these large-scale meticulous maps as a tiny black square
is today a brush-grown hole or depression. Stone walls
grope through timber as thick as your thigh; pathetically
faithful lilac shrubs keeping alive to make a dooryard;
dying appletrees as clues to ancient orchards, but over-
topped by birches, maples and oaks. All that is now left
of generations of pioneer sweat and struggle. Porcupines
extending their range into the valleys; deer tracks abundant
on the neglected roads; residents here and there sticking it
out say it is almost impossible to keep chickens in the face
of the abundant skunks, foxes and weasels.

Another straw in the wind is that, recognizing how much
farm land is being neglected, every State north and east
of Maryland, except Maine, has started a campaign of long-
term conservation, trying to induce as many rural owners
as possible to reforest such tracts. It is far better, the forestry
commissions urge, that useless land be planted to evergreen seedlings, than that it should become northern jungle;
cat brier, blackberry, struggling thicket.

✿   ✿   ✿

THE NEW AMERICAN WILDERNESS

It is indeed high time we started to do some walking.—
Away from the locked garage. Walking, the exercise, is
quite distinct from Walking, the hobby, the pastime. Nothing set down beyond this page has anything to do with
walking as exercise, *per se;* let us leave health out of this!—
Or take it for granted; knowing that while a long war is
going on, a maximum of personal effectiveness can come
in that long run only through true relaxation, changes of
pace and of thoughts and interests; brief interludes though
they be, between worries and fatigues.— If only that and
nothing more. But Walking can be something more. Properly pursued, usually is.

Everyone readily agrees that "walking is good for you"—
as exercise. Sometime, probably, a majority will *do* something about it. Possibly shoes for feet, *for use,* replacing
shoes for manikins, will come into style again. General
agreement already exists that Constitutionals, *i. e.* turns
around the block, or the park, or down along the river, are
probably "good" enough to expiate a lot of self-indulgences.
But that walking in general, besides being surprisingly good
fun, is passport to an empire of hobbies, a soviet of enjoy-
ments, remains yet a sort of FBI secret. Foot locomotion
in the following pages is presented under slightly different
guises and varying aspects — as you will see — but under
them all it is always self-entertainment.

Where is the land of Luthany,
Where is the tract of Elenore?
—I am bound therefor.

Pierce thy heart to find the key;
With thee take
Only what none else would keep;
Learn to dream when thou dost wake,
Learn to wake when thou dost sleep;
Learn to water joy with tears,
Learn from fears to vanquish fears,
To hope, for thou dar'st not despair,
Exult, for that thou dar'st not grieve;
Plough thou the rock until it bear;
Know, for thou else couldst not believe;
Lose, that the lost thou may'st receive;
Die, for none other way canst live.

When earth and heaven lay down their veil,
And that apocalypse turns thee pale;
When thy seeing blindeth thee
To what thy fellow-mortals see;
When their sight to thee is sightless;
Their living, death; their light, most lightless;
Search no more —
Pass the gates of Luthany, tread the region Elenore.

—FRANCIS THOMPSON: *Sight and Insight*

CHAPTER IV

BY NIGHT

I FEEL certain that were I to suggest that long walks at night — as long and varied as a daytime tramp — through meadows, pastures, woods, are even *possible*, many would utterly doubt it. Were I to insist that one *could* "see much of anything"; that night walks hold a great deal of intriguing interest; are full of novel nature encounters and of aesthetic impressions of a high order; most hearers might be openly skeptical, or gently indulgent toward a poor chap's queer notions of pleasure.— Well, I make these assertions now — and am *not* taking the defensive.

Night life in the country, the sort of life I mean, is caviar to the general — must always be. How will you know whether you are general or private if you do not make the experiment?

From the vast amount of print, film-footage, and chatter about it you might well assume that the exciting pastime called night life was confined to cities.— By no means whatever! Great activity goes on here in the country; plenty of entertainment — if one cares for the type.— No lack of human interest. Or sex appeal, for that matter. Walking at night around the countryside is truly one of the keenest of delights. Night is yet as unexploited and unexplored a place as "the region Elenore" of Francis Thompson's poetry. . . .

One Summer afternoon I found on a tree trunk in the woods a large and beautiful moth, a particularly lovely object, all downy yellows and umbers and rich grays, and a disk of blue upon each underwing. A glance identified it as

[39]

NOW THAT WE HAVE TO WALK

Polyphemus, a virgin female of the species, which had just emerged from her silken chrysalis in the dry leaves on the ground below. Slowly, slowly like a gesture of breathing, the four wide wings fanned up and down, drawing life into themselves, circulation, feeling. Expanding, strengthening, erasing the hundredfold creases into which they have been crumpled in the silken oval out of which she came.—A worm, a huge bloated, tuberculed, hideous caterpillar went last Autumn into that cell; from it had resurrected this soul-like thing. A symbol now of Psyche awaiting there the touch of Cupid. Psyche preparing for the great adventure; ready for it, nearly, garbed in fine raiment, knowing instinctively of the things to come as they had always, always come to her ancestors for over a million years. . . .

I gently carried home the beautiful maiden and released her inside the screened porch. Ten feet was the span of her first flight in the world; it ended as she settled like thistledown against the wire screening and clung there, unfearful, unexcited, confident; a shape of perfect form and exquisite color. . . .

Night came on. Outside, cricket castanets kept up a cease-less bolero; the soft wail of two little owls in the shrubbery lent an eerie kind of violin obbligato; frogs in the near-by pool played bass saxophones. Hundreds of fireflies far over-head twinkled on and off like some fairy signboard against the mysterious velvet background of the dark. I sat in the shadows of the porch to watch what might happen. And I waited and waited. . . .

—Ah, she was the Princess Polyphemus no longer! But a Circe wafting a spell abroad. Unknown to the watcher, undetectable by his dull senses, through the shrubbery, over meadows, deep into woods, was drifting the ineffable aura of love. To distant mates with supersensitive antennae it had spread, though there passed very little breeze. Miles away the tiny fern fronds caught that signal and straightened themselves; aroused wings began to flutter, at first gently, quiveringly, uncertainly; then aloft, wildly ascending into exploratory circles, trying to set a course toward the source of the magic spell. Presently these lovers drew nearer and nearer, following the evanescent odor as fogbound aviators ride their radio beam.... One soft projectile after another came thudding against the screen. Two, four, eight; then four more. Oblivious of everything else in the world, the male moths threw themselves at the baffling barrier. For somewhere near, the unseen Circe was luring them; her presence pervaded the air. And now, as if stirred by the soft thudding sounds, yet not taking flight, her own wings began slowly to move; her body gently quivered.

I sat astonished. In all the years I had lived here I had seen only two of the species; now there were a dozen Polyphemus Lochinvars out there under the stars! A frenzy of beating bodies hovered about the one spot where she clung. They crowded against one another in the air and on the screening, and occasionally the collision of their wings could be heard. What a passionate quest! Theirs was a veritable dervish-dance in its abandon; they were hypnotized by a spell they had never felt before and never would again.— Which of the twelve would Fate choose? — Should the suitors be let in; should the enchantress be sent forth?

—But look! A larger shadow has cut through the blue-gray dark! A sharp click as of two dry twigs struck together. Another darting shadow; a second click.—What *are* these shapes?—Ah, the owlets from the garden trees! Now the erstwhile dance of love has become a *danse macabre*. Murderous shearing beaks have stopped the rapturous rigadoon, quick slaughter scatters the whirling performers.

All Circe's witchcraft is powerless against this! Her suitors are seized in swift succession; snatched from her at the brink of consummation.—Will not *one* survive those cruel executioners?

The porch light snaps on. I dash out to drive away the owls. At my feet, like rusty autumn leaves upon the grass, lie a score of severed wings. Am I too late for the rescue? No. For there against the wire yet clings one of the twelve. The others have risked their all for her — and lost. It is as in the old fairy tales where bold young princes must defy the cordon of guardian ogres to snatch away the lovely captive; and genii and spirits come to the heroes' aid. Sole survivor, he shall gain admittance to the castle! — And in the role of Destiny, I lift him gently off the screen and take him inside the porch. . . .

Brief sanctuary. Brief existence. For him and for her all that life beyond the chrysalis can hold is love. Such is the adult Polyphemus's one purpose. Mouth, throat, stomach, functionless; neither food nor drink nor travel in the sunshine are theirs who leave that silken capsule. Only wings, in order to seek like this or be sought. To fail or succeed that perchance the race survive. . . . Hardly here may we distinguish night life from night death. . . . The cricket castanets still click; the saxophone of the frogs has not ceased; the fireflies spark on and off; only the violins are muted and missing.— On with the dance, the wine of life yet flows — down another street. . . .

All this interplay of beauty and brutality, of creation and destruction has unfitted me for sleep. By now the moon has risen, floodlighting the countryside into a stage effect of noon. A sense of mystery is all about. I decide upon a four mile walk by the wood-road over the mountain and back. "In such a night as this did Thisbe fearfully o'ertrip the dew and saw the lion's shadow . . ." — *No, no,*— On such a night as this rubber shoes are the thing; that one may pass as quietly as wild feet do. Down the orchard lane,

[*42*]

across the scrubby pasture to the forest edge. Man wandering thus at night is a sort of wraith, a spirit in a spirit land, completely out of habitat, fulfilling no practical purpose, gaining no biological end; like a fish out of water. (Which, no doubt, is the feeling of many a man in a cabaret!)

As well as I know my way about in this little cosmos surrounding my home, I go stealing around at night as ill-adapted as a caged bat.—A bat! My spotlight picks it out of the dim air a moment, just long enough to reveal that Mistress *Fledermaus* is carrying a tiny young one clutched tightly to the fur of her breast — a sight for night eyes, indeed! Now she is vanished, utterly dissolved in moonshine; into the trees perhaps to park her helpless burden tidily upside down on a twig so that she may forage and bring it insects with greater freedom — for such is one of her maternal practices.— That zigzagging bat must spend *at least* three-fourths of its existence dead-to-the-world, shut-eye; yet manages during the night hours to carve out something of a rounded career! An easier conscience it gives me that my own one-third of a lifetime is spent in bed.— Unconscious for eight hours every day! How much we miss of marvel and surprise by night, as does the bat by day.

It is never *very* dark outdoors at night, contrary to a widespread idea.— Never *pitch* dark. It has long puzzled me as to where so much illumination comes from on a starless, cloudy night. In my own much traipsing about, I have almost never been out when I couldn't get around readily; when I could not see the ground under me; see obstacles, get over fences, jump brooks, descend rocky banks. Recently, in the process of training aviators, it has been learned that humans have a true night vision, though it is not very powerful in most men. The ability to see in the dark comes through an ocular equipment different from that used by day,— something like the owl's retina which in the human eye starts functioning after some quarter of an hour in the dark; so that many can see far better than they ever had occasion to notice that they could.—"The night-pilot after flying for an hour can see a candlelight twelve miles away, even if it were exposed only for a thousandth of a second."

Darkness, of course, merely *conceals* outdoors and does not change it; everyone *knows* that. Yet despite mental awareness of so simple a fact, most of us find it almost impossible to eradicate entirely a deeply ingrained *feeling* that night is night and day is day. Different in tempo, different in quality. Down through the centuries men have built up an immemorial tradition in which there persists a vague expectation that at night we may encounter strange, unheard-of creatures, supernatural things, weird aspects of plant life, even alterations in the topography. I cannot to this day shake off such a foolish belief without an effort. How the poets have put the fear, the fancy, the romance, the unreality of night into us! I recall vividly an evening long ago when the astonished realization came over me for the first time while seeking a cow in a familiar woods: why, *everything*, trees, brooks, paths, hillocks, *is exactly the same* as it was this morning!

But it is really not quite the same. Science says that the leaves are now "resting," asleep in a fashion, as are those flowers which close at evening. In the dark the wood-tissue or cellulose of the growing plant is being made from the raw materials manufactured in the sunshine by the leaf's green chlorophyl-bodies.—Also, another insect-world is actively functioning, the day's world is quiescent; night birds, night animals take the place of those busy by day.... A slight sound startles me! A mere hint of a gray something seems to move there, there at the left of the path! I tug the flashlight from my pocket.

I have been climbing the mountainside wood-road; here

it crosses the brook noisily gurgling down from a spring-fed pond in the woods.— Yes, *something* over there! I direct the strong beam upon it: two yellow coals glow back. — A raccoon. It is squatting on a rock, and pauses, startled, transfixed, in its occupation: the washing of a succulent-looking frog in the stream.— A frog, of all prey, to need sousing in the water out of which it has just been snatched!— Yet every coon mother's son and daughter performs this dainty and seemingly unneeded ablution of its food. Never had I seen a wild coon actually doing it. My spotlight blinks off and on, on and off; still no movement. What insoluble mystery must this be to the performer staring into that beam — it must seem like a nightmare; I continue to concentrate the illumination on the raccoon at the water's edge, several seconds elapsing before I begin exploring with it the forest depths behind. A slow rotation of the light — and lo, four other pairs of eyes glimmering yellow from the dark! Four infants have accompanied mother on her tour, and there await their portion of the frog. Whimsical, peering, comic masks of faces; woolly, ring-tailed youngsters only half-grown! Now directing the beam steadily into the mother's eyes, I creep toward her. Blinded, she does not move. The dashing water blanketing the rustle of my footsteps and clothing, I come within arm's length. I stoop — and actually disengage the frog from her claws! She whirls with a little cry, stumbles toward her brood and stampedes them into flight. They all go crashing into the undergrowth, the light catching them in a score of poses, until they finally vanish beyond its terrorizing, ghostly fingers.

On and up. Now *feeling* with my feet for the narrow path; overhead leafage is denser, little light reaches the ground. My passing awakens a sleeping Wood Peewee on some unseen bough; there comes a faint call of protest, irresistibly drowsy, a soft fading fall of sweetness long drawn out.

NOW THAT WE HAVE TO WALK

Then almost across my very face slips the ghostly passing of a Flying Squirrel, the gentlest of all God's creatures, as it glides from one tree to another seeking — *what* imaginable things in this lonely Stygian gloom which it knows as life!... Then, all at once, lights through the trunks; level, distant, shining straight into my face: the bright horizon stars. I emerge upon the barren, shale-spread one-time pasture, its broad hogback — whaleback, rather — the summit here of my tame mountain. Tame? But only a little. Men tried to tame it over and over when the republic was younger, but either their whiplashes or their tenure were too short. It is true they dropped the trees and brought the bed-shale up through the forest mold; so that at length no loam is left and today little or no grass can penetrate the "soil," and noon heats wither most of its growth by June.— That would be taming of a sort.... There above they are, as they always were: The Dipper, Polaris, Arcturus, Vega, Altair, and the rest of the celestial index-points. There yellow Saturn, there red Mars, and flashing bright Jupiter, *bright enough to cast my shadow!* Faintly, but yet a shadow, as my waving arm attests. The Milky Way inscrutably hazy, a vast belt of primal fog — the fog in which we forever move! Amid almost utter quiet I stand, at first hearing nothing; then begin to detect that low steady blanket of sound which one has to listen for in order to hear; "a sound so fine that nothing lives betwixt itself and silence." But it is not close by here; it comes from a distance, from below where the night chillness is a few degrees less cool. Uncannily quiet, nevertheless.... Behind me far away in the woods below a fox barks once, twice; mournful? eerie? — or is it just a normal fox statement of fact? From off to my right where I know the little hemlocks are creeping, creeping into the shale-beds while nobody is ever there to watch them or halt them, comes the alarmed "sneeze" of a deer — she has caught on a zephyr the scent of man! To make sure all her clan has heard, she repeats the odd signal — and then it is heard no more. . . .

I stood a long time still, and listened.— Always I enjoy listening; by the sea, in the April dawn, across the snow at sunset; and I cannot get enough of it; it is more exciting to me than seeing! I *am* seeing life, nature, the world *through another sense*. . . . A curious obsession, is it not, that man lays so much emphasis on seeing, so little on hearing or smell? As animals, we are all virtually eye-minded, like cats and owls, whose eyes like ours look straight ahead; pursuers all. Dogs as a rule are primarily scent-minded but possess good eyesight too. Rabbits must be ear-minded. All vertebrates which are pursued view a 270° arc, or nearly so, having poorest vision straight ahead. It has come to pass that we humans feel we have not *really* identified a bird or insect or animal until we have "laid" eyes on it. . . . So intent are most of us on our ready eyesight, that earsight has to be struggled for. Yet it is easy to "train" the ears; musicians must, outdoor-explorers can, and it is highly remarkable how much one's hearing may detect by effort, and how enjoyable it is; in effect not unlike scanning a wide panorama from a height. "Acuteness" of hearing is usually only marked familiarity with and interest in that which is listened for. The soothing effect of silence is well known — such as that during Winter nights in the country or in depths of evergreen forests after a heavy snowfall. . . .

And now down again to the places of bed, board and bath. And the end of what is undoubtedly the deepest and closest communion with Nature which most mortals can experience: A walk in the night.

✿   ✿   ✿

NOW THAT WE HAVE TO WALK

—Did I not say it: plenty of night life here; a change of
attractions nightly; no cover-charge — whatever that is indoors — in this countryside of mine; and no rueful "morn-
ing-after"! — Yet candidly it must be stated that night bird
life is meager; animal rovers then comparatively few.
Almost none of the Reptilia move. If one counts Woodcock,
Night Heron, Screech Owl and its several larger cousins,
and the Whippoorwill; the list of Eastern States' birds is
finished. Check off the raccoon, skunk, Flying Squirrel,
opossum, the moles, some of the mice, these comprise
almost the census of nocturnal mammals. (Foxes are out
a good deal — *too much!* — at night; but prefer a degree of
moonlight and not too heavy a dew.) Many animals commonly regarded as nocturnal are really "crepuscular," *i. e.*
twilight-haunting. Bats are crepuscular, as are the smaller
rabbit tribes, these feeding mostly during evening and
dawn, though at courting seasons and in late-Winter moonlight they are somewhat more reckless of the hours. Rabbits
know instinctively they must retire early; (as do Gray
Squirrels and Red) that except in March mating season
they cannot for the life of them afford to be unwary of the
big owls that hunt all through the night.— Though once,
at 10 p.m. in June, I *did* see a woman walk ten paces and
pick up a rabbit, a wild one, while dazzling it with a flashlight!

Crepuscular only are the Whippoorwill and Nighthawk
(not a hawk at all); both cease flying at "pitch dark," except
that the former does fly a little and *whip* all night in nesting
time. Comparatively few night animals work the whole
night; I think that porcupines are as thoroughly all-nighters
as any. For them, certainly, all night and no day makes
life a dull joy; less buoyant, more doleful mammals probably
do not exist. A few common mammals not normally nocturnal have been forced into the practice by their proximity

to man and his works. Near human haunts Muskrats stir about almost wholly by night, but in removed regions I have known them to be busy all day long. Beavers too adapt themselves to the safety-first demands of their lodge-site; working at night in some spots, by day in others. In Adirondack depths they go around openly in the daytime. . . .

—Is a city's "White Way" afire with a million electric bulbs? Well, a quarter of mile path alongside my own meadow-brook flaunts more than a million, maybe five million, lights, *and not one advertises anything.* That spectacle — a country commonplace — on a hot June evening — if it were seen but rarely in a lifetime, would thereafter be spoken of with quickened breath. If stared at, the flashes dazzle one like electric arcs; brilliant, perhaps they would be blinding if they persisted several seconds. I have always thought it odd that so little is written or said about this wondrous thing. Sometimes a city person who comes up here is almost overcome by the beauty of it, having been quite unaware it existed on such a scale. The Japanese are much more concerned with it than we, for when the display is at its height at Uji, special trains are run, thousands come from big cities; at least, they did when I was there. But that was some years ago B.P.H. After we have beaten down their war lords and "aristocrats" we might consider starting such a custom here. . . . The light-efficiency of firefly illumination greatly exceeds that of anything man has created; sunlight is but thirty-five per cent light, an electric arc ten per cent, gas about three per cent; but "lightning bug" light is between ninety-six per cent and one hundred per cent light-rays! Presently city dwellers may catch up with us by synthesizing this natural lighting and using it in place of electricity.

Almost anyone who goes about seeing things at night will add an extra set of puzzling questions to the usual crop picked up by day. For instance, does that mother bat find her young only by hearing, after she has hung them up in the gloom of the foliage? How do they themselves learn to catch insects, for even adult bats cannot *see* many of them they catch in the dusk of evening? How can they watch the way mother catches them? Is all that adult dexterity possible only through *hearing* insects fly in the night sky? Some say so. You will see a bat drop twenty feet to seize an insect. (Blindfolded bats can fly about in a room experimentally crisscrossed by strings, and never hit one!) . . . What do female mosquitos drink if they do not chance upon mammalian blood? In Summer there must be a mosquito to every square rod of non-mountainous America. Hereabout you cannot sit outdoors of an evening and count fifty before one arrives. Mammals to puncture are not that common. Do you think, rabid as they are for your veins and mine, that the majority of these feminine vampires are to be satisfied merely with plant juices (as some students insist) — or with nothing, like the stingless adult male mosquito? Does their obvious and rabid greed for blood make that seem likely? — Why, oh why, can they not all be entirely content without blood!

Where and how do nocturnal creatures get contact with those ultra-violet rays we hear so much about, and which make us produce Vitamin D for ourselves? Do they ever absorb any at all? Do most night creatures get Vitamin D from eating day creatures and/or green leaves; or do they manage to spend some part of their life basking in the sun the way the raccoon, opossum and rabbit do? Would these last two be so very hearty — and prolifically fertile — if they did not in some manner absorb plenty of Vitamin D?

The nocturnal opossum can produce more young at a birth than any other American mammal. Up North here they are becoming ever so much commoner than when I was a boy, and no wonder; sixteen and eighteen young at a birth is not too unusual. On occasions, a mother has been caught with a dozen or more graduates from the pouch riding upon her back while another litter of a dozen or so were living in the pouch! There's quantity-production from the night-shift for you! If rabbits can multiply arithmetically, 'possums seem able to do so by geometric progression. They have this birth-rate business down to an exact science: "when newborn," says William Beebe, "seven thousand opossums are needed to weigh a pound . . . instead of remaining unborn for several months, the infant appears in the outer world after only eleven days, helpless, shapeless, more like a great pink grub than a potential backboned animal. (It) possesses one perfect thing: an inborn instinct to creep or crawl in exactly the right direction, two or three inches to the waiting pocket. And not only this, but it has to climb upward all the way and at the end of the journey nose out one of its mother's dugs. Its eyes remain tightly closed for six weeks, but that pouching instinct is as unerring as if rehearsed for a lifetime."

—But *why* are 'possums coming to northerly latitudes so recently? They survive a Winter's severity around my home, seemingly with rare casualties. Why then did they not cover the continent hundreds of years ago? Why should we always regard them as a Southern curiosity, linked with negro cooking and persimmons?

If one stops to think about it, he realizes that nearly all extensive orders and families in America contain at least one species going in for nocturnal living.— Sort of a black sheep, as it were. There is a night butterfly; day-flying moths are nearly as numerous as the night species. Nocturnals appear amongst the salamanders, crayfish, frogs, felines, canines, weasels, rodents. And in a family often there are light and dark "sets" of species: day and night

[51]

supplements to one another: owl and hawk, katydid and grasshopper, Flying Squirrel and Gray; toad and frog, moth and butterfly, skunk and red weasel.— Odd fact about frogs: that they appear to be both diurnal and nocturnal, eating in daylight, apparently spending the whole night in wassail and song. Since neither occupation is too arduous, this burning the candle at both ends apparently undermines neither their fertility nor their health.

In your walks in the moonlight across hill and dale you will probably begin to notice three optical illusions. One is that the moon which looms so huge and spectacular when lifting above the horizon is very much larger then than when it swims overhead. Another is that "it is nearly as light as day!" under a full moon. The third is that hills, dunes, mountains, trees are huger and higher by night; that ravines and hillsides are deeper and steeper. True or false? All three can be easily debunked. Hold a pencil at arm's length and measure the rising disk along it with your thumbnail; then do the same again when the moon is overhead. As to the second, look here and there a moment underneath trees or shrubbery or at a stone wall; you see in a flash that your moon is no sun. The proof of the third problem lies in common sense. The reason for the illusion is the same reason which baffles a person in the first illusion: namely, that without a familiarly known, tangible object to serve as a reference-body, one's eye simply gets rattled about sizes and shapes. At the horizon are trees, perhaps houses, to compare the disk with; dunes, hills, ravines, are so isolated from surroundings because of the dusk that here too one lacks familiar reference-bodies. A bird in a fog or against a bank of mist looks disproportionately large; I have mistaken a robin for a crow, and at a hundred feet. Again, your reference points are missing.

How many reference-points in the night sky astronomers

have pointed out for us! We should be thankful for these, for otherwise the vast vault would seem Chaos itself (—which, indeed, it may be even to the oldest and wisest astronomer) with no place of beginning for any nomenclature of the stars. One may hardly deem himself even superficially familiar with starlore or be satisfied to think he has measured his soul by a cosmic yardstick, if he does not "go forth under the open sky and list to Nature's teachings" (as Bryant urged) — that means, in simpler words: make a practice of taking walks at night in the country. Rightly enjoyed, astronomy can never be an arm-chair or textbook study.— Who would contend that without astronomy the attainment of full spiritual and mental maturity were at all likely?

Occurrence of Northern Lights is a far more common thing than is generally suspected. Displays of a faint sort take place several times a month; oftener in Winter and Fall. These are so varied in form and colorations that consecutive ones are not apt to resemble each other. Many auroras are so low-powered that from a village, city, or even an area near a lighted house, they evade notice. Also characteristic is an almost constant fluctuation in intensity; even on the fieriest evening come intervals when no hint whatever would be caught were not the full scope of the horizon visible. When an especially brilliant aurora develops, out here where houses are strung along roads as telephones on a ten-party line, the word flashes quickly around: "Go look at the Northern Lights!"— And we run out and then as like as not we run in again to call some friend miles away.

That overwhelming exhibition through the evening of September 18, 1941, in my experience the most spectacular by far, possibly caused more local telephoning than Pearl Harbor. Even now when I recall how nearly I missed seeing

NOW THAT WE HAVE TO WALK
that one, I resolve anew never again to go to bed without
a careful scrutiny of the sky. In all probability I shall not
look upon its like again — actually, there *could* be a rival
this week, *tonight! — If I were to miss it!* On that evening
several of us lay upon our backs in a dew-soaked clover-
field and watched for three solid hours while all the fire-
works displays of all the Fourths and Bastille Days put
together were being outdone. As for myself, I actually
trembled a little, almost uninterruptedly, not from chill
but from the inner excitement I could not express in movement or noise. I felt within, a sort of fear-not-fear which
must have been the workings of *awe*, a state which so rarely
overwhelms one like that. At midnight when we went to
bed from sheer weariness, the sky still remained a miracle.

I believe it futile to try describing such a night. Especially
so, in that one of the remarkable *sequillae* was the strange
divergences in the descriptions of it which circulated next
day. I grew more and more puzzled the more accounts I
heard. To me the Great Aurora was mainly characterized
by this-and-that, not to mention numerous minor features.
But no. Others spoke breathlessly about effects we failed
to recall, or recalled as secondary, merely transitory details
on the vast lightscape of the heavens. . . . Yet one memory
I must record. It is yet vivid after more than two years.—
That the almost constant flashing effects, whereby pulsing
illuminations like lightnings seemed to *flow swiftly inward*
to the zenith repeatedly and repeatedly; seemed to dart
in along some kind of vast celestial screening which remained *fixed and there;* persisting from flash to flash, from
minute to minute, as though it were a permanent network
or background far, far up into the stratosphere, above and
beyond the color displays themselves.— No one has ever
mentioned to me noting such a thing; such an inexplicable
"mechanism."— Could I have caught, by any remote chance,

[54]

a glimpse of that "framework of the Universe" into which Thoreau preferred to drive the nails of his ultimate philosophy, "rather than into the lath and plaster" of ordinary living!

Every leaf and twig was this morning covered with a sparkling ice armor; even the grasses in exposed fields were hung with innumerable diamond pendants, which jingled merrily when brushed by the foot of the traveler. It was literally the wreck of jewels and the crash of gems. It was as though some superincumbent stratum of the earth had been removed in the night exposing to light a bed of untarnished crystals. The scene changed at every step, or as the head was inclined to the right or the left. There were the opal and sapphire and emerald and jasper and beryl and topaz and ruby. . . Such is beauty ever — neither here nor there, now nor then — neither in Rome nor in Athens, but wherever there is a soul to admire. If I seek her elsewhere because I do not find her at home, my search will prove a fruitless one.

—HENRY THOREAU: *The Week*

CHAPTER V

IN WINTER

WINTER emphasizes stark reality, never bemusing one into the kinds of Fool's Paradise one often inhabits during warm seasons or in tropic climes. And for natural life it is no season of jollity and snug conviviality. Its cold makes all living things come to terms; causes hibernations and migrations. Vital topography is streamlined, so to speak. Leaves are off so that wind may howl, snows pour down, with least damage and danger. Winter's cold is real and menacing; life forewarned, must prepare for it. The most complete adjustment and change of which living things, animal and vegetable, are capable, are accomplished in order to meet our annual Ice Age. Cold tames the snake, the turtle, the amphibian, and some of the mammals in spite of their burning blood.

"The way reptiles seek winter protection is particularly interesting," writes Raymond Ditmars. "They are cold-blooded; a snug nest would mean little to them, for the temperature of their bodies becomes cold as the ground grows cold. Snakes are the most particular, though, as they are the most delicate. They must seek places where there is no chance of freezing temperature penetrating. They must be safe from the ground becoming deeply frozen. . . . They never take a chance. They do not simply go into holes or clefts in rocks for winter shelter. Always, for the serpent clan, there are certain places with which the snakes are familiar and to which they return year after year. How they find their way to such places is more or less of a mystery, scattered as they are during summer over far fields and woodlands. Their sense of direction in returning to the

NOW THAT WE HAVE TO WALK

hibernating dens through grass jungles, labyrinths of rocks, through swamps and ravines, is as marvelous as the migration of birds. The places they go to are called "snake dens," where crevices go deeply beneath the surface — twenty feet or more. Here in clusters they go into a dormant sleep from which they awaken with returning warmth of the spring sun. . . ."

In many ways this general adjusting to Winter is a kind of recapitulation of the adaptations life must have tried to make when the last Era of Ice began slowly whitening North America and Europe. For one thing, the seed-mechanism, developed quite recently as geologic time goes, is obviously a device for conquering Winter conditions. Essentially seeds are quiescent plants without freezable liquid and with starch (which cannot be dissolved out and into premature action) substituted for the chemical sugars (which *must be* dissolved with aid of warmth in Spring) from which renewed growth is built. . . . For another thing; a self-defensive torpidity, of short duration, which might have sufficed for the brief chill periods — later to develop into true Winters — at the onset of glaciation, has today persisted into being what we know as the long Winter-hibernation in mammals, insects, amphibians and others. Hibernation, then, would be a trait passed down through the *survivors who retreated.*— Who did not sleep until the ice closed over their heads forever.

There appears to be no evidence from geological records in stone, in sands, in fossils, that there was any such phenomenon as alternate Winter-and-Summer; until our most recent series of Ice Ages began their several retreats; say, about forty to a hundred thousand years ago. Winter is something rather new in the lifetime of the earth! Inasmuch as there were in distant ages, long before this recent one, three or four major Glacial Epochs, it is thinkable

[58]

that for a time before and after each, Winters occurred
regularly. But no record tells that surely. And the biology
of organisms which survived those times appears afterwards
uninfluenced by such yearly alternations. . . .

As for our turtles and amphibians, they "migrate" into
mud-and-water below the frostline and wait motionless for
Winter to blow over. Of our mammals the woodchuck is
soundest sleeper and longest. The Black Bear rarely hiber-
nates south of latitude 42° 50′. Skunks, coons and chipmunks slumber more fitfully, especially the foremost. A
skunk slips into brother woodchuck's or sister rabbit's burrow about Christmas, but checks out before February is
half over. Practically all other mammals stick it out in some
way or other; asleep only by night. Bats migrate — at least
from New England, New York and New Jersey latitudes.
Few insects survive unless they be in chrysalis, or have in
larval or adult form crawled down below frost; but
their eggs live — as do plant seeds — and therefore the race
lives.

Here in the East in Winter distances increase, landscapes
lengthen. Taking it by and large, the walker equipped with
binoculars projects himself a good ways and can detect
almost any movement; thus sees more per leg-mile than
at any other season. No distraction from insect pests; only
the sting of frost and bite of cold. Foot-locomotion now
may turn in as high a rate of interest on time invested as it
does when more living things are about. Almost the only
creatures which habitually hide with success are hare and
weasel; turncoats which in late Fall wear white.

To the alien walking visitor during the six bare months
of the year the appeal of a landscape can be notably different from its greeneried aspects. His general estimate as
to its attractiveness as a place to settle in perhaps, or to
explore later on, differs flatly in Summer and Winter.— Of

course, main contours of topography remain fixed perenni-
ally; yet, as Napoleon is said to have muttered on stark,
volcanic St. Helena, "Who can live on geology!" In Summer and Fall few regions in these rugged Eastern States
are not attractive. Despite the unmentionable number of
Winters through which I have lived, and the divers spots
in which I have lived them, even yet I am too inclined to
optimism, too fondly hopeful of an area I visit when its
foliage is on. From indications drawn from the sort of farms
which city folks purchase up here, I judge this to be a
general, widespread failing.— Never buy a country home
during the Summer or Fall! One brought up in the East
must go West, or South, or to Canada and the tropics to
grasp the slightly surprising fact that grass, green grass
over some eight-twelfths of the year, is the East's priceless
prerogative. Green meadows and pasture lands, green
swales, hills, mountainsides, are features of relatively few
populous areas of the globe; though many areas do enjoy
brief benedictions of verdant ground. . . .

Painters seem generally to agree that for illuminations,
for subtle effects of light, Winter snowscape is richer than
Summer landscape. For ethereal, fugitive interplays between
earth and sky; for lightings which often descend upon you
unaware; they say, watch Winter dawns and sunsets! In
general, this light-magic seems to depend little upon cloud
formations and reflections therefrom, as it does at other
seasons; but something more of the quality of wide *atmospheres* is in them. I assume that to make the most of these
Winter light-effects one simply must own or acquire the
painter's faculty for analyzing and composing colors; a
faculty which, it would appear, is oftenest the outcome of
years and years of study, learning and practice; and not
something blessedly inherent in temperament. Rockwell
Kent has brought us from lands of perpetual Winter holy

[*60*]

gifts from out that faculty; he has returned bearing atmospheres and awe. . . .

The nature lore of Winter in the Northeast affords, of course, sparser fare than will later in the year be served up, and was served to us but yesterday. For a novice, the walking appeal of a country road or woods in Winter depends in great part on what species of bird and animal he sees — not very many; what tracks they insert into the record as evidence; together with his ability to identify trees and shrubs in leafless woods and fence rows. Trees in Winter (— by the way, there's a good book with exactly that title!) present difficulties, inasmuch as most of the published aid rests upon their Summertime details. No difficulty about the *coniferae*, they remain evergreen (except the Larch). But, I imagine, to most beginners all other kinds look bafflingly nevergreen. . . . As for birds to watch for and check off, the usual listings of residents inland hold but about twelve; the rarer visitants being Goshawk, Pine and Evening Grosbeaks, Northern Shrike and Snowy Owl, with some six others numerous and widely distributed. Identification of animal tracks is relatively an easy matter; several good illustrated works settle virtually all questions. Having mastered them, perhaps fifteen in all, thereafter along your pathways whenever snow conditions are right, unrolls an unposed, never-ending, never wholly repetitious newsreel or action-picture packed with human interest. The dramas, truly serious and not make-believe, will entertain you upon even the dreariest and scantiest of terrains. Yet obviously the human trailer must through practice become able to read the trails he sees. Hollywood scripts notoriously oversimplify life; likewise with these snow-stories; in the main brief, plain and to the point, Nature seems often to make life and death in them oversimple matters.

NOW THAT WE HAVE TO WALK

Yet I recall one "feature" of which I could not say that its motivation was revealed then, or now; or that its narration was exactly clear. It was unrolled before me several Winters ago.— Winters, I said, yet the time actually was mid-March; the Winter character of it consisted of one full foot of fresh fluffy snow which had descended without warning all the previous afternoon and evening, while we were, figuratively speaking, "sitting in the lap of Spring"— or supposed we were. It had been an unexpected, unseasonal foot of snow; dramatic in itself.— As was the tale it disclosed.

That morning about daybreak I waded across the vegetable garden to examine a line of deep wallowings in the snow some thirty yards distant, which from the kitchen windows suggested the passage of several deer. These wallowing tracks, when presently I stood over them, completely baffled me. Not deer's at all. For some ten minutes I studied them, going back and forth between the house and the woods, before I told myself finally and out loud: "These footprints I have never seen before!" I stood there, carefully calculating, checking off impossibles; until all that were left were beaver — and otter. From knowledge I possessed up to that moment, these tracks could not have been made by either.

It would be impracticable here to describe the topography locally and that in the vicinity; so I may state only that on the southern side of the long east-west single-fold mountain (under whose lee we live) no beavers could exist for twenty miles; but that, beyond our fold to the north, is a large stream paralleling the mountain, in which several beaver colonies were now living. Yet what conceivable reason for beavers to climb — in a heavy snowstorm — over a stubborn, steep, rocky mountain, come down on this side, then turn about and go back; all in one night? This was no

Spring emigration movement, a beaver-pair exploring for a new place to settle. — Far too early; Winter as yet hardly routed; most ponds still ice-covered. . . . Then, then — *otters!* Otters, however, had not been reported from this whole region for a generation.

Though breakfastless, I began to warm to my work. In a few minutes of wading around, up brook, into woods and return, I added three items to this legendary adventure I had stumbled on. First, enough clear footmarks to establish otter identity — these positively were not beaver. I saw that wherever the slope of the terrain permitted they had slid down on their bellies, legs trailing, making long round-bottomed troughs. Second, the route across the garden was their *way back;* while along the course of the brook, some yards upstream, another trail was the route of their *coming.* The latter, because slightly dusted with snow, was obviously the earlier trail. And, finally, that a third otter had joined the others on their return at some distance up in the woods, it having for some reason made a wide detour around my home.

A brief summary of what four sweaty hours of tracking, mountain climbing and descending showed — before the clear morning sunshine effaced the record and closed the books — was this: For reasons obscure, three grown otters — rarest mammal in the southern half of the State — decided to make an exploration and outing combined, enjoying the exciting novelty of a soft-snow storm coming in mild weather.— Only to see what they might see? Only to play in the elements like a gang of small boys? Who knows? . . . About dusk, short-legged, waddling and wallowing, they left the bank of the creek far down across the mountain from us. And crawling through nearly a foot of snow, ascended the rocky wooded slope to its ridge, a matter of over a mile; zigzagging so freely, so pointlessly that they doubled the distance. They did not follow a watercourse although several do tumble down the mountainside nearby. Reaching the summit, they came shortly to an artificial pond several acres in extent. It was icebound except for melted openings along the edges. Into this pond they dove, passed under many rods of ice, and one, at least, emerged at a little dock and sat there to eat a fish. At length they all departed from the water at its outlet, and down this watercourse they came, at times sliding, skidding like boys at play; until they reached the modest headwaters of our own brook; about which all is pasture land. Near this point one otter left the others, turning far to the east it crossed a pasture and went on down a road — how far was never learned; nor why the separation. The two followed our brooklet for over a mile, finally coming to the small river which carved out the valley in whose broad windings we reside.

The ground distance covered in the night by the animals from creek to river could not have been *less* than three and a half miles. All their traces were lost at the river-brink. . . . Then, a few hours later they started back, following about the same route by which they came; mysterious Number Three joining en route at a wide angle. The snowfall had now ceased, for the trail back was distinct. I continually received the impression that their whole excursion had been great fun; was in fact, just-for-fun. Yet perhaps they were also exploring — but *for what* here among the farm lands? Repeatedly the snow revealed what looked like sheer romping and poking about. Repeatedly, as I said, they slid from three to fifteen feet where possible.

The sliding habit of otter is characteristic and well-known; in Summer they are fond of plunging down rock-slopes into pools among the native fastnesses where they live. Here, they slid in snow like sleds, their legs parallel to bodies. One could detect how extremely sleek and slippery they were, for they slid upon grades whereon only a wet fish could slide. Otter fur is the *sleekest* of all furs, more so when wet.

Now *why* this seven or eight miles in a night? I hazard not even a guess.— Here's "A Winter's Tale" for you! Otters coming right down your little woodside brook and through your vegetable garden! I have reason to think that probably no human being in the State knew of their existence. . . .

—Any more than I had known of the existence of Collembola, apostle of the Abundant Life. Which is another story on the snow.

If I had been harboring doubts (and I believe I had) as to whether vital fecundity retained its primeval potency; or if I had suspected that because *Mammalia* and *Reptilia* were steadily becoming smaller and smaller as geologic time unrolled; that because *home sapiens* itself had exhibited almost everywhere a shrinking birth-rate, Mother Earth was well past her climacteric; Collembola reassured me on these points, revealed to me a hint of the power this universal protoplasm stuff is capable of; showed me life without stint or limit; life unutterably abundant; life apparently without the faintest rhyme or reason, so far as human affairs go.

If you should wish to see also what I saw last February 23rd, you would have to look for it during that rather barren season when Spring is but half-guessed by faint auroral flushes sent along the wavering vista of Winter, when late Winter is just merging into early Spring — the time when otters, for instance, "longen to gon on pilgrimages"— in that period, I mean, when snow crusts at night and by day becomes slush.

On that kind of a morning about dawn, I entered a wooded area, half rhododendron swamp, half mixed hard-

wood and hemlock forest. Suddenly I noticed that the old
snow underfoot appeared to be dusted with soot, as though
it had been receiving the outpourings of factory chimneys.
For some minutes I walked along, absently speculating as
to how this snow ten miles from any such chimney could
look like that. Presently I observed that all small depres-
sions, especially old footprints made days ago, seemed the
dirtiest, as if the soot had been drifted into them by wind.—
By that time I developed presence of mind enough to get
down on my knees and really look at those black specks.—
Those specks were alive! Some among them constantly
jumping about. All jumping like mad when a finger was
thrust near. Here was a "black snow"; something to match
the famous "red snow" of the Rockies, of which everyone
probably has heard. This was animal "snow"; that other
effect caused by a plant, a red algae.

I lifted my face in awe and looked about. This blackened
surface stretched away as far as I could see — and it was
alive with infinitesimal insects infinite in numbers! *Acres*
of them. And the hand which had sown them there had
made each of them perfect. Yet so small were they, the
magnifying-glass from my pocket revealed but meager
details. Insects they were, of course, but of what family?
genera? species? I had never known of this astounding
thing! I walked on, through a half mile of this wonderland,
and yet it came to no end. And started from no beginning.
For it was a sort of *seasonal* layer of life, covering a *region*:
a phantasmagorial parade *of a species*. Each time that I
stopped and made the glass play upon the black dust again,
there under it were hundreds of six-legged vital mechanisms each perfectly, cunningly formed. Smaller than the
smallest snowflake, as finished and finite as a flake; no more
so, no less. Beneath my clumsy soles a gigantic social world,
emerging from eggs, courting, fighting, mating. I could see

[66]

all this on the sterile, chill surface — which to them might have been the Glacial Age surface itself. Had I winged among the stars in the dead cold of space, I could have beheld no greater inventory.— And as humbling, was this gazing upon birth, life and reproduction on a scale so Lilliputian, so astronomical, so aloof.— What's man to them; or they to man? . . .

If you look into this most terrifying thing, books will tell you that these are earth's smallest and most primitive insects.— Of the Order Aptera (wingless ones), Class Collembola (Spring-tails), Family Sminthuridae, Species S. aquaticus (perhaps). Yet can the great Classifiers tell you what niche in the Scheme of Things Entire these animalculae fill? — And why they dare presume to outnumber all men, all mammals, all vertebrates put together? — As if the earth were intended particularly for them to enjoy, to exploit, to inhabit abundantly.— For that is just how Collembola apparently regard this world —"of *ours*."

Were you to imagine that I exaggerate their superhuman mastery of their environment; their awareness of "life, with all it holds of joy and woe, of hope and fear. . . ." I would like to go back eighty years and quote you from old Sir John Lubbock, who virtually founded the science of insect psychology (He is writing of Sminthurus luteus): "It is very amusing to see these tiny creatures coquetting together. The male, which is smaller than the female, runs around her and they butt one another, standing face to face and moving backwards and forwards like two playful lambs. Then the female pretends to run away, and the male runs after her, with a queer appearance of anger, gets in front and stands facing her again; then she turns 'round, but he, quicker and more active, scuttles around too and seems to whip her with his antennae; then for a bit they stand face to face, play with their antennae, and seem to

be all in all to one another."— *Multum in parvo!* S.luteus is
not a millimeter long.

*   *   *

The "average person's" vagueness about cold and about
Winter cold, are two odd phenomena. We grouse at a chill
of 25° in November, which truly we welcome as a "hot
spell" when January comes. In February and March at
some 12° we work and walk about coatless on sunny days,
whereas if we had to face it two months previous, we would
bundle to the eyebrows. And, if one pauses to reflect, the
fidgety concern some members of one's family express
when the house thermometer in the living-room *drops to
62°!*, is amusing; for at 62° next April the same member
will be humming Mendelssohn's *Spring Song*, and all the
doors will be open.

Undoubtedly the said "average person" used to our Summer and Winter ranges of temperature, which can run from
40° below to 100° above, would be incredulous if he were
told: "There is no reason to suppose that the earth's average
temperature during the last Ice Age was more than about
ten degrees colder than it is now . . . 10° mean annual
temperature is the difference between Cape Cod and Cape
Hatteras. . . . A drop of 3° would probably put back the
glaciers of northern Scotland." The foregoing is quoted
from *This Puzzling Planet* by Professor E. T. Brewster,
an established authority on geology. . . . He says elsewhere
in the book: "An Ice Age is a local affair. . . . Greenland is
ice-capped still . . . we don't really know that the Ice Age
has ended, nor that the ice is not shortly coming back."
Ice Ages are apparently not due to cold so much as to heavy
snow which does not all melt during Summertime. This
being true, a certain scientific basis lies beneath the stock

answer which my parents used to make to a stranger's asking "how the weather is up here?"—"Wall, we have about six months Winter and six months sorta late in the Fall. And we don't get much sledding around Decoration Day.". . .

Until around 1920 skis were as rare in these States as rickshas; in consequence Winters were largely indoor interludes for all but the hardiest pedestrian fanatics. Luckily some five years ago I learned to ski; since then a part of my own Winter Walking has been replaced by skiing. Skiing *is* Walking, of course — as is indeed bicycling — walking de luxe; walking in high-gear, as it were.— On levels and on downslopes; but, oh, *not* uphill, when on both the effort certainly becomes Walking in *low*-gear — if not at times "in reverse." Now, practically anything which may be said of Winter Walking as a pastime applies as well to skiing. . . . Skis at length took me to the Catskills, the Greens and the Adirondacks, areas which in Winter are effectively out of bounds to all foot walkers. Until skiing began to suffuse through the population, these and similar preserves were no man's land from around December 1st to April. Today, to skiers, there is no place at all, however removed, hid from the sight thereof.

Truly, skiing and bicycling are forms only of Walking — new steps in the Dance of Life; each is locomotion under your own steam. Your *own* steam! — Meaning movement through your *own* volition, cranked by your inward self-starter.— Meaning, further, organic, individual participation in one's own self-entertainment.— All of which, I hold, to be part of a highly imperative strategic retreat to the old, quieter base of operations where physiological upkeep and refitting are possible for personalities and temperaments battered, shattered, tattered by machinery, its noise and speed.— Yet at times secretly I tremble with pessimism.

NOW THAT WE HAVE TO WALK

Observing how and with what universality gasoline-powered ski-tows climb and cough; young motorists and old drive *to* skating ponds, *across* lake ice, *alongside* golf courses, *into* outdoor cinemas, *through* "motor savings banks," and *by* natural beauty; I tremble lest, this War over, we may not see a kind of winter-jeep invented and used to ply the snowy ski-slopes in more modern style. These, loaded with a new type of athlete, will ascend, reach the summit,— then, quick; clutch out; a shift from low gear to *skids;* and *down the run* on its set of double skiis; swift, swift, as though it were charging a pillbox or establishing a bridgehead.— And all the occupants will have skiied de luxe, sans exertion or risk — or any participation at all!

* * *

By the grace of skis I have learned to know another Adirondacks. For years I walked through the mountains in Spring, Summer, Autumn. Yet longed to traverse them in Winter and to know those places where men did not go. Except in Winter, it is all but impossible to travel such a wooded wilderness unless you keep to known trails and wood-roads, for the forest floor is half concealed by undergrowth, utterly uneven, spongy and treacherous. So dense is Summer's foliage that visibility through the green gloom is often less than a hundred yards, while the mountain landmarks can hardly be kept in sight. From hour to hour their very identity shifts into conjecture, just as their positions come to occupy quite illogical directions.

In Winter when the floor is flat snow and summits are visible, it is almost impossible to get lost; if skis are the means of locomotion you may launch into the white forest wherever you will. Impossible to get lost, did I say? I hasten to add, unless snow starts falling. Should the flakes begin

[70]

coming down densely enough to cloud the distant outlook, beware, for real danger can come in a twinkling. Being lost in a mountain snowstorm is no humorous situation. Your wits and stamina must be pitted against time and distance. Probably — as in Summer, if lost — you will start swinging 'round and 'round in wide circles, coming again and again upon your all-but obliterated trail. Possibly you cannot be sure which direction these tracks are going. In a predicament like this you must do what a plainsman lost in the dark does when he lets his horse have its head: let the skis carry you down, always down, for this is your surest way to safety. In time you are bound to reach a road; a road means a house. . . .

The wild things of the inner Adirondacks do not expect man in the five white months. This is a clear impression gained after a little exploring on skis. Animals are less on the defensive; alertness has given place somewhat to endurance. During these weary weeks man as a menace takes secondary rank to weather — to cold, snow, sleet, blizzard, and to the hunger and hurt that come out of them. Since the creatures are not expecting you, at times they appear almost indifferent to your silent unmenacing human presence. You see deer as you never see them in the other seven months; they live differently, in most respects eat differently.

One "yarding-up" place I used to visit was rendezvous for about fifty deer. It was in the shadow of Mt. Marcy, some four miles from a road. And this is as near as conscientiously I can reveal it. Though they do not do so at other seasons, deer for several reasons herd in numbers together in Winter and establish a yard in some food-favored place. Though not a wolf now survives throughout the whole State, herding to fight off wolf attacks was doubtless a prehistoric necessity; hence an ingrained habit now. Again, it is difficult for deer to move swiftly through

[71]

NOW THAT WE HAVE TO WALK
uncrusted snow deeper than two feet. So from the beginning of Winter they proceed to keep open a maze of trodden paths in which they can walk or run no matter how much snow accumulates. In addition to deep snow, one of Winter's dangers is that the fragments of a thinly *crusted* surface, too light to bear an animal's weight, may injure a running deer as would blunt knives, cutting or bruising their fragile legs. The mechanism of a deer's hoof-and-hock joints is peculiarly liable to injury. Damage, however slight, to their thin, steel-sinewed limbs must be avoided. The yard paths, therefore, serve as open highways and as a vast labyrinth in which to elude enemies.

This particular yard, a dense growth of young spruces on a brook-flat, could be approached so silently, and from leeward without being scented, that I could watch deer after deer jump from the snow-hollow which was its bed that morning, and go stiffly along some trail of the labyrinth centering in the fastnesses of the spruce thicket. By mid-Winter under nearly every sapling there came to be a packed-down ice mattress on which a deer had repeatedly slept.

What a wild life community center that ten-acre yard was! Tracks of grouse, foxes, lynx, weasels, minks and hares were everywhere. Along the sluggish brook on the further side, muskrats used to crawl out briefly from beneath their ice roofs, and apparently almost every day three or four beaver living farther downstream came rollicking up through snowdrifts and water, perhaps to hobnob with the rats. It was a Winter notable for deep drifts; at the end of February evidence piled up that the yarders were pressed for food. Practically every young balsam had its twigs denuded as high as a deer on hind legs could reach. And all shrub browse such as witch-hopple, dogwood, osier, viburnum, and hardwood saplings, were

[72]

nibbled off; even followed down into the snow a foot by
hungry muzzles eager for more. What possible nutriment
resides in balsam needles is hard to understand, yet deer
can if obliged survive on them alone, it is said. Conifer
foliage is usually eaten, however, only in times of necessity.
At other Adirondack deer-yards foresters hung out cakes
composed of suet, bran and molasses; but at this removed
spot my deer were strictly on their own.

After a fall of light snow the skis sometimes bumped
straight into hares and grouse which had dug-in and sought
temporary warmth in soft, fluffy drifts near this yard. Out
they would flutter and blunder about until their wits and
muscles began to function; I have taken spills to avoid
crushing them. Nature outfits both bunny and bird every
Fall with a set of true snowshoes; those given the hares
are of heavy, matted fur, the grouse get a web of crisscrossed bristles between the toes and around the outside.

I made many nature contacts that Winter; was accepted,
or ignored, and could observe birds and animals at close
range. One day, slipping along a forgotten trail which only
in Winter could be noticed, perhaps a trapper's trail of
twenty years back, I began ascending a ravine. The lightly
packed snow made skiing perfect; my progress must have
been practically noiseless. Happening to glance ahead
through a clearing where many young spruces were half-
buried, tufted or smothered by new snowfall, I saw a lithe
white creature dart under one of them. Was it a weasel
dressed in its Winter ermine? I had but a tenth-second view
and was not sure. A jiffy afterward a Snowshoe Hare burst
from the opposite side of the little snowy tent. Before I
could guess what was happening, a weasel followed, seemingly intent on capturing that hare. The big bunny, not
noticing me standing motionless thirty yards away, again
disappeared within the cave-like tunnel beneath another

[73]

NOW THAT WE HAVE TO WALK

tenting evergreen. On came the weasel, its thin body alternately curling up and straightening out in a series of swift leaps directly in the wake of its swifter prey. Out shot the hare on the instant and hopped along to a third disappearance, this time well towards me. The wicked little demon followed. Neither paying me the least heed.

"Why is this going on?" I was asking, "he'll never catch up with that rabbit!" Then an answer came; a flicker of movement at my very feet. I looked down to see, leaping directly across my skis, a second weasel! Two jumps distant, its evil snout and red eyes pointed up into my face, it stopped a moment to stare, malevolent and fearless. It paused to size up this tall shape it had never seen the like of before; then paying no further heed, turned away, stood abruptly upon hind legs, sniffed the air with quivering nose, and peered and peered ahead.

These two hunters were working together! One was working to drive out the quarry, the other was to lie in ambush and make the kill. Silent and motionless on my skis I watched the game of life and death. The dumber-witted hare, easily bounding away at safe removes from weasel Number One, obviously did not realize the danger which lay ahead. Instead of fleeing into the distant forest reaches, so far that no half-yard-jumping weasel could ever catch up, deluded bunny was now, as if contemptuously, watching that tiny white pest, kicking back long heels at it as she easily bounced ahead toward danger. The rabbit was now circling, coming near me all the while. And close by me crouching low, watching, watching, nearly concealed by a spruce tuft, waited Enemy Number Two.

It was not a long wait. The denouement came more quickly than I expected. The rabbit paused again to look back. With two swift springs Weasel Two was upon her and seized her throat. In an instant both were there, and a

[74]

squealing, kicking bundle of gray-white fur soon lay still. Impelled toward revenge, I pushed forward and sliding right upon them tried with a ski pole to strike one of the defiant little beasts. Whether due to the kind of stance the skis gave me or whether it was just weasel magic, I did not once land a sweep of the stick within a foot of those dodging weasels! They would not run away. They gave ground a bit; waited and watched; closed in when I stopped lunging; dodged or leaped over the next stroke. I simply could not hit them. After another minute or so of excited effort, I gave up.—After all, why should *I* seek revenge? This bloody affair was *natural;* that I should be a witness, mere accident. No, no affair of mine; nor was it pleasant to watch further. I slid away. . . .

A week after this, I struck a fresh lynx trail far below and was following it over a high saddle on Moose Mountain. I have long harbored curiosity as to just what kind of place during Winter a wildcat calls home; there was a possibility that this trail might lead me to some kind of den. On the further side of the ridge the lynx trail had turned into an open wood-road leading down, and I began "snowplowing" and straightening out, alternately, in order to slip slowly along.

About me everywhere was the beauty of height, of primeval forest, of mid-Winter. A score of distant peaks could be seen under a raiment of spangled sunshine in regal majesty. Silence was queen of that high white realm so remote from the world of man. The only sounds my alien ear detected were the faint lisping converse of chickadees, the occasional silvery chatter of passing pine siskin flocks, at rare intervals a lone little woodpecker's feeble tapping. It is incredible that such birds live for months in this icy Eden, thrive on its sterility; keep spritely and friendly towards one another, despite the chill bitterness of the six-

[75]

NOW THAT WE HAVE TO WALK

teen-hour nights. These rugged birds are so self-sustaining and impersonal, as aloof from man as are the Dipper's stars! As I glided slowly downward in the silence I suddenly saw something coming to meet me. It was a tawny lynx bounding lightly up the wood-road; not floundering, not even sinking much in the snow. The creature was dragging something. What? I stood still; a man at the cat's distance probably would have noticed me; but it did not. It came on, up and up the long rise of the road. I was amazed to see that its burden was — *a white duck! Where* had that been captured! The laboring cat came on, breathing hard; passed me *within five feet*, and disappeared around a bend. It had neither seen nor otherwise sensed that I was there!

I have yet to see a wildcat's Winter domicile. But I learned next day that a famished lynx will come right out to a barn in daylight, claw its way through a stuffed-in windowpane, bring back a duck through it, and get away to the woods, despite a man and a rifle. . . .

I could not possibly catalogue all the experiences of my days on skis in those secret and silent places. I may have covered a hundred miles in all. I never needed to run the same course twice. The silence of my movements and the help of my binoculars enabled me to hear and see what life was stirring, and what ever changing beauty the inner wilderness was providing. Over bottomless swamps, up and down surfaces of streams, narrow and broad I could now go. So effortlessly! On some days a sense of freedom akin to that a bird must feel impelled me on and on beyond my strength; I would hardly admit fatigue. Until nightfall, when the West faded to indigo, the stars slipped out, the great tree-boles began booming and snapping under the bitter squeeze of the cold. . . .

For walker or skier, truly there is "nothing much to see in Wintertime"— unless you go out and look for it!

[76]

AFIELD AFOOT WITH CHILDREN

Introductions

Waxwings and lichen and red cornel fruit,
Deer-buck and hoot-owl, gray granite and newt,
Hedgehog and deermouse, the drumming grouse cock,
Junco and cedar and spring-from-the-rock,
Moosewood and bellwort, clintonia pale:
This is my brother, the north mountain-trail.

Blueberries and redstarts, squirrels and brier,
Brown hare and laurel, logs with fox-fire,
Ferns and the killdeer, the dogwood and pine,
Caddis and glow-worm, the pink eglantine,
Trout and the wag-tail, crayfish and leek;
This is my sister, my sister, the creek.

Blue sky and blue mountains, blue rain when it sweeps;
Blue like the gentian, the blue ocean deeps;
Green pasture, green meadow, green forest, green lawn;
White snow and white daisies, white frost at the dawn;
Gold-rod like gold sunset, a gold empire's-worth:
This is my mother, my mother, the earth.

Red-snake and sora, the arum of wax,
The wren and the bittern, the musquash-lodge stacks,
Snow-lily and bullfrog, the blue pickerel-weed,
Gas bubbling mid tussocks of wild rice and reed,
Dragonflies planing above the green scum:
This is my father, the marsh — whence I come.

Shingle that's pounded with foam, hiss and roar,
The gull and the skimmer, seaweed on the shore,
Deeps that the tortoise and jellyfish own,
Shark, whale and lamprey, the pink coral-stone,
Rocks barnacle-stuccoed, half-smothered in brine:
This is old Ocean, godfather of mine. . . .

AFIELD AFOOT WITH CHILDREN

THE 18th of April. 9 A.M. An Eastern State. A woodland whose floor is carpeted with hepaticas, adder's-tongues, claytonia, hellebore and a score of springing things; whose brooksides are brilliant with marigolds; whose glades and thickets ring musically with new bird songs; whose ponds chorus with hyla pipings "like a ghost of sleighbells in a mist of snow" . . . I had just returned from three hours of exploration — and had encountered not one human being. Yet along one edge of this "wilderness" runs a concrete highway bearing past 2000 cars in an hour, and in that hour one of them could have transported me to a city half as large as the national capital.

I cannot get used to it; I will never understand it: this waste of Aprils. Squandering them — the bare two score of them — as though human life were eternity! How few adults treasure their few Aprils as they do their bonds, gold pieces and diamonds, or spend them with equal plan! Yet, undoubtedly, one of God's greatest gifts to us is an April dawn. Few of us, after reaching twenty-five, find time to look full in the face one Spring sunrise or to know what a single April day can bring forth.— Is not something amiss with a civilization which ignores nature as we do? All but a small fraction of the daylight hours of our grown-up lives are passed indoors; much of it only to acquire possessions which tie us down rather than free us. Surely it is simplicity in living, individuality and independence of mind and of person; intimacy with biologic reality, which tend to free us. We are truly not free unless we are doing most of the time the things we want to be doing most. Simple or

AFIELD AFOOT WITH CHILDREN

"barbaric" people live better; reality touches them at more points than it does us. Even our forefathers lived more vitally, vigorously, more at first hand. Our calendar, seasons, clocks, holidays, weather, the practices of sowing and reaping, religions, marriages, seafaring and such, derive from nature, earthly and solar; though we moderns are unmindful, if aware. Our contact with nature's phenomena which make life and civilization possible, is shadowy, make-believe.— Can we afford such aloofness?

Too many of us "must," it seems, work in offices, factories and such confining places a lifetime; shuttle back and forth tiresomely over the same routes; give almost as much regard to dress as if ever hoping to be hired as manikins to pose in life's show-windows; and in the scanty spare hours left, go in for something gentle like golf as a kind of expiation for a misspent youth.— Or we swim, motor, dance, read, attend theatres, concerts, travel abroad, travel everywhere,— seeking happiness. Finding it sometimes, often not; rarely realizing until our forties that the Holy Grail is hidden in the wayside weeds just across our own drawbridges; unaware that "rank, office, title, wealth and all the solemn plausibilities of the world" are hardly to be compared with foot freedom on chosen mornings like these.— Always I shall wonder what wages buy, so precious as the birthright of going outdoors when you want to. What satisfactions and rewards indoors, abed and asleep, are to be had as fair exchange for thirty mornings in forty Aprils. . . . "So many Aprils went away before I learned one little part of all the fragile joy each hid in its heart."

As to what concern all this is to me, I cannot answer. Unless that it springs from an inherited taint of evangelism. And if the foregoing seem to be a jeremiad in the Minor Prophet manner, forgive me! But I assure you it comes from no hermit sitting in the market-place crying "Woe to Jeru-

salem!" Rather, it is a preachment from the temple itself;
a voice calling out of the wilderness.— Come forth with
me on some April morning that I may tempt you with
something better than a hermit's locusts and wild honey....
Why April, rather than the other eleven months? Well,
April is preeminently the nature lover's month, despite all
the romantic popular songs about May and June. It is then
easiest to fan into blaze the lingering sparks of an instinctive urge towards wildness, which all children, at least,
transiently possess. Easiest for several reasons. The outdoors is full of invitation. The cooped-up days of Winter
are past; a moderately warm day with clear sky is a novelty.
On certain such days adolescent Spring seems suddenly to
have grown up, to put on, as it were, last Summer's cast-
offs and to parade, coyly, self-consciously, up and down the
drab countryside.— That odd restlessness called spring
fever, what is it but a vestigial call in man corresponding
to the stronger impulse which turns wild creatures definitely towards migrations and matings? — Easiest, again,
because the woods and fields are open, unobstructed; ap-
pealing to eyes and to feet. Undergrowth and thicket are
not yet in leaf, and reveal most of the secrets entrusted to
them by last year's insects, birds and animals. Bramble and
fern are crushed flat. Cocoons, nests, runways, dens, the
creatures themselves, have little to hide behind. Nature
lays her cards on the table. Before the May leaves come
out, life among the early migrant and resident birds is
completely at the mercy of one's binoculars. Since relatively
few showy flowers bloom in woods after tree foliage begins
to shade the ground, the best flower displays there are
over by the middle of May. No insect pests appear during
April. Marshes, swamps and surface pools teem with
interest; hylas, frogs, salamanders are there, croaking,
fifing, mating, depositing eggs.— Hardly a shred of excuse

for such of us as shyly say, "I *do* wish I *knew* something about nature — and had a chance to get outdoors along with the youngsters!"

—On the contrary perhaps you've been saying, "My children just don't care about that sort of thing."— Well, how *can* they if they live in Urbia or Suburbia and never had a pin prick of encouragement, but are probably copying your own reluctance? Does anyone enjoy skating or swimming if he doesn't know passing well how to do either? Inevitably we are shy and self-conscious before the thing which is not familiar; so apt to take up with what we are taught — subtly, indirectly taught — the national game, the popular pastime, the current style — and to regard the ways of the minority as queer.

Perhaps to you April is just a calendar month. If you do not comprehend my enthusiasm, perhaps it is because early mornings have become to you only a series of zero hours. You are used to having your day begin with breakfast time. Nature may have become "a far countree," as foreign as Madagascar. If you dwell within a city of six figures there is much reason for that, and, alas, little to be done about it. Yet, townsfolk and small citizens; even those of you who may not have seen a sunrise these twenty Springs; you are certainly missing something, and so are your children. . . . Overcome your shyness; break the ice.— this is my plea. Learn How to Make Friends (outdoors) and Interest People (yourself)!

If you were to ask me at this point for an opinion as to what chiefly is "the matter with" the younger generation, I would have to reply (as I did at length some pages back): "The same that is the matter with most of their parents; trying to build a life around sheer *entertainment* — being *entertained*, I mean, by somebody else." What has this fact, if it is a fact, to do with nature hobbies for children? Why

NOW THAT WE HAVE TO WALK
is nature study one of the good bases on which to build
for a zestful life?

Because, for one thing, nature interests demand active
participation and *not* passive acceptance. Because it involves mind as well as body. Because someone else's skill
cannot play a major part in them. Because they lead easily
into the sciences and invite deeper understandings. The
pursuit is exhaustless and can be continued throughout a
lifetime wherever one may live. And a penetration, at some
angle of — let us call it: outdoor biology — is possible to
anyone. Almost without money and without price — as the
Bible says about salvation.— Maybe, by the way, it is a sort
of salvation itself. . . .

"Come out with me some April morning," I said.— For
something better than locusts and wild honey — though
wild honey is about the best treat there is. So here you are.
There are four of us: yourself, your Mary aged twelve and
your Billy of ten. In the very April of life themselves!

We have parked the car — or was it bicycles you came
on? — in a woodland lane, and, most intelligently wearing
most unrespectable clothes, are knee-deep in April before
even the sun is up. Bill has an empty market basket over
his arm, Mary a pair of two-quart Mason jars fitted with
wire handles for the occasion, a ten-cent-store kitchen
strainer for dipping; you carry the field-glasses and the
trowel.— Not a sound more than is absolutely necessary—
each of you have agreed to that!

Being novices, you are each a little disappointed that
the first ten minutes are not more exciting. Down along the
path (which, unknown to you, is leading us to where
Mother Woodcock is brooding her eggs) you keep gazing
about into the early twilight, listening eagerly; but presently thinking: "Well, I don't see that there's very much
going on around here; I'm afraid it's not going to be very

interesting . . ." But that is simply because you do not as yet understand. . . . I show the three of you a two-inch hole going under the roots of a maple and tell you that the snow record a fortnight ago proved conclusively that on two consecutive mornings a Weasel dragged a mouse from the swamp grass nearby into the snug ancestral den below. Now this innocent hole reveals no secrets. That same last snowfall likewise disclosed that two skunks regularly hunt throughout this apparently deserted vicinity; and that it is home to a Muskrat, many Whitefoot Mice, squirrels galore, a pair of foxes, at least one Puffed Grouse, a 'possum, several newly resurrected chipmunks, rabbits by the half-dozen, and a lone Snowshoe Hare beside.— Nothing to see? You had better keep looking. . . .

Let's sit by the spring here until the sun is above the ridge. Arbutus is in blossom, that's what the exquisite odor is in the air! Is there manufactured any scent to surpass this one which is distilled out of a moldy, mossy bit of April turf? The almost-level sunshine suddenly gilds the beech boles around us. It is a signal. A score of different bird voices awaken. A Waterthrush whistles rapturously every ten seconds along the brook; a tabloid Winter Wren on his way north bubbles forth ecstasy enough for a bird 5 times as large; a chorus of Robins begin caroling in unison; a Bluebird pair warble back and forth a melting tender love-song. Just beyond the treetop screen a Red-shouldered Hawk is screaming as it circles over the nest where its mate is incubating three or four heavily marked eggs. Flocks of Redwings and Grackles, ready for another long northbound journey, are making a great racket before starting. Chickadees and Nuthatches cannot seem to express all they want to say, and Flickers, just arrived, repeat breathless long-winded alarms from all directions. The air is all music.

NOW THAT WE HAVE TO WALK

Mourning-cloak Butterflies, one of the first spring insects to emerge, have left the leaf heaps into which their larvae crept last autumn, and are trying out the faint yellow warmth of the sun. Comrades in earliness, the little blue Spring Azures are here too in numbers. The wildflowers common to April are countlessly spread before us; and cinnamon ferns which will presently do their part in transforming this spot into a baffling summer tangle of secrecy, are pushing violin-headed fronds up from each of last year's clumps.

But we must get on, to surprise Mother Woodcock on her last day's vigil at home.— She is at home to us; there she sits. I have difficulty in pointing her out, so perfectly does her back marking blend with the dead leaves and sticks among which she made the nest. Billy is able almost to touch her before she flies. Four handsome mottled eggs. No nest. A mere hollow in the leaves. The last snow fell upon the sitter's back. . . . I feel I know a good deal about this particular Woodcock pair; in a way. Yet, in reality, I can know so little. For eleven years a pair has nested in this vicinity, and every Spring night, beginning about March 15th, the male has performed his wonderful evening flight-song above a certain small clearing near-by. In Aprils I have found either eggs or peeping little chicks; in Winters I have flushed them from watercourses and spring holes and have seen their tracks in the snows. But after all, what do I know? — is it the same pair these eleven years? What is behind that stirring flight-song which fifty times a night, eight weeks in the year, takes the little performer gyrating up into the evening sky, chirping, twittering, as round and round he goes like a skylark, then lets him drop like a stone to the earth at the very square-rod from which he rose? It is not a courtship, for it lasts far too long. It is not done to keep a sedentary bird's wings fit for the great migration

[84]

flight, for these birds move South by short stages only, and then not very far South. Perhaps it is just for joy-of-living. To seek answers to such questions as these, is both the delight and the duty of a naturalist.

In the space of these pages we cannot trace each step of our morning. In detail we shall not relate how Billy, climbing a fifty-foot pine to look at a nestful of infant crows, found instead that the place was inhabited by a Red Squirrel family whose youngsters scattered to the four winds on his approach — all but one which tumbled into our hands below. We are unable to picture Mary knee-deep in swamp water, leaning over the top of a muskrat lodge and looking into its interior through a hole in the thatch, where, she said, five young rats were nosing from under the mother's sleek sides and wondering what next.

However, we have reached the starting-out place again, and here are items of our booty: Roots of the ten earliest wildflowers in our basket; same to be set out in the woods garden at home; and a few fern clumps as well. A huge bouquet. A baby Red Squirrel tied in a handkerchief in my pocket. One quart jar packed with Spotted Salamander egg masses; the other with four hylas, a pair of newts and several hundred Wood Frog's eggs about to "hatch." A collection of perhaps twenty cocoons of the Prometheus Silkworm Moth all of which were hanging upon one spice-bush shrub. A Red-eyed Vireo's cup nest, charming architecture hardly damaged by a year outdoors. A series of regurgitated Screech Owl "pellets" (felted ovals of mouse fur, feathers and miscellaneous small bones) also carefully wrapped in a handkerchief for home inspection under a lens. These we found on a wall where Screecher was wont to dine.— And, oh yes! four sets of thoroughly soaked feet and legs, which wetness will never do us any harm.

So much for tangibles. What else? A knowledge that

[85]

NOW THAT WE HAVE TO WALK

trees usually have their largest limbs towards the south and that only where trees stand far apart do they preserve their lower limbs at all. Knowledge that salamanders are not lizards; that crows, hawks, owls and the woodcock may start their nesting even before the last snow has fallen; that Wood and Black Ducks are commonly feeding in woodland pools during northward migration; that Garter Snakes are rather fun to handle and do not object to it; that a frog cannot breathe if its mouth is held open; that Honey Bees are as much at home in a hollow tree as in a hive; that Flying Squirrels do not fly but can coast several rods when startled from holes in a dead stump overhead; that a Song Sparrow has not one but a whole repertoire of different songs.

These things are by no means all we have observed and learned. We have learned how much we do not know; how much there is to find out; how challenging are the meanings underlying habits, markings, colorations, shapes, appendages, food, life cycles, interrelations, rarity; as found everywhere throughout the world of plant and animal. We have been immensely *entertained* — but, astonishingly enough, we have been entertaining ourselves! We find ourselves trying to delve into principles and vital generalizations. The great school of the out-of-doors has caught our interest; it is educating us unawares. The whys of Nature are related to the whys of human life. . . . You *can* take it all with you!

THE FIRST WEEK OF MAY

Wild Goose Feather

There it was by the spring —
A quivering wild goose feather!
Though he had not seen a passing wing
In the wild Spring weather.

Lost from the punctual wedge
As it had driven on,
The feather stirred in wind at the edge
Of his pasture spring at dawn.

He knew that many things,
Elusive, above the mind,
Left something, as these unseen wings,
In season, for him to find.

Something that he could touch,
Excited, then be content —
Though it could not be possessed too much
At the edge of wonderment.

—GLENN WARD DRESBACH

THE FIRST WEEK OF MAY

SOME dozen years ago I attended a performance of Turgenev's *A Month In The Country*. I clearly recall *the fact:* I did go. Enjoyed it. Forgot it shortly. That I remember *having gone* is due to no reason intended by the playwright; not to the acting (which I am sure was flawless), nor to the cleverness of dialogue and character delineation, nor to the plot — but to *the superb irony of the title.*— A petty memento to carry away and treasure all these years, you may think. I am not sure. At least, I have held ever since a great respect for Turgenev's genius simply because of it. And I continue to feel that this very irony gnawing in his heart was the reason he started writing that play.— What was this irony? That all the characters were so utterly alien to the country which they had come out "to enjoy." The country bored them. To the symphonies of a rural Russian Spring, with its multiple variations on the major theme, these fine folk were tone-deaf. It was all Chinese music to them. They were veritable city-prisoners, and prisoners of their class and its stylized living.

Now the supreme Week of all weeks here in central New York State covers the first seven days of May. That this period in the country could conceivably bore any one of my fellow citizens normally equipped with sense organs, and with any reasonable degree of familiarity with our great green cornucopia of a world out of which comes pouring ceaselessly life, life and yet more life; I am not able to grasp.

If I were imprisoned for life, though allowed freedom during one week every year, I know that I would choose the first week of May. For, taking it year in, year out,— though it fluctuates a little forward and backward occasionally — it is *the* week for nature lovers. True, those particular days are never *long enough* and they vanish into the past with unparalleled quickness; yet I would choose them. . . . Come to think further about it: why, a great many people are all but *imprisoned* — in a job, often for what amounts practically to life sentences! Indeed, I happen to know personally four such; three men and a woman, all past fifty, who have held only one position in their lives, and though each receives a monthly salary to spend, each was (to my way of looking at it now) surely sentenced to and is serving a lifetime term.— Not in solitary confinement nor at hard labor; but held under a sort of parole-and-curfew system by which each must report every weekday at 9 A.M. and not drop out of sight until 5 P.M.—And, yes, each *does* have an annual free period, though it happens to be *two* weeks long. (— I never grasped all this before! It is most remarkable.)

May 1st, then, for freedom. (— Strikingly that it is Labor's Mayday of Freedom, too!)— Not that on or about May 1st Spring begins.— Nor that "sumer is icumen in" so early.— Nor that any sudden change occurs then. For that matter, Spring may *come* or *go;* no man knoweth whether or when it happens.

Then what makes the first announcement of Spring; who or what brings the First news? Our calendars on March 1st say it is — technically, astronomically — just ahead of us, just around the corner. But *how* near is it — just when will Nature's Spring start? A very odd, persistent confusion as to when it gets to be "really Spring now" crops out annually in the newspapers. To a naturalist public "news" on Spring is invariably stale. It would seem that no one who writes the papers holds any idea of what, when, and where Spring

is. Yet they do write about it; people seem to like to read about it. And *why* do so many of us, busy at desks, in shops, factories, homes, care about this thing? Why does a primitive, primordial sleeper awake in us; perhaps all of a sudden on a day when we happen to notice the resurgent sun is high toward the zenith already? Is it faintly vestigial instinct — or nostalgia? Thoreau once answered thus: "Measure your health by your sympathy with morning and with Spring. If there is no response in you to the awakening of nature, if the prospect of an early morning walk does not banish sleep, if the warble of the first bluebird does not thrill you, know that the morning and Spring of your life is past. — Thus you may feel your pulse. . . ."

Notice that the sage of Concord does not say "the first robin," but "the first *bluebird*." Yes, it is usually so; the latter is far likelier to fetch "the mail of the season" up this way. The Bluebird is the most impatient of the migrants reluctant to go, eager to return; I have heard and seen bluebirds during every month of the year. Yet, in fact, what a tardy postman he is. Spring's first messages will long since have been delivered before you catch that gentlest warble from the blue this year. The skunks have received their notice. After a snug hibernation, not entered upon until around Christmas, they have rubbed their weasel eyes, uncurled tails from around sensitive weasel noses, judged the time by the looseness of the pelts on their thinning bodies; and set out upon forages across the crusted snow.—Ah, perhaps it is the crusting of the snow which is the earliest harbinger. Before scentful little Mephitis has set foot upon it, it would bear him. And shortly will work its topmost layer and its southern exposures into a lacy coverlet patterned by the noon sun's warm needles of light. It is only February then.

Even by this date, however, the very earliest of sun

worshippers will have begun hereabout the rites of Spring:
Great horned Owls will be incubating eggs — they take
turns, each of the pair, in doing so. No egg-layer undomesti-
cated by man rivals the female of that species in anticipat-
ing the season.—To lay eggs, in a tree-top, before mid-
February! That even in this region these huge owls feel
the love-urge in January and bring forth young before
March 15th, is astonishing. A nest of only bare twigs,
seldom with lining material of any sort; often with scarcely
a hollow; is a *home* of a sort. Snow warmed into ice by
their sitting bodies often surrounds — and *underlies* — the
pair of billiard ball-like eggs; yet the devious ways of
biology take their course. I recall that in 1934 the first eight
nights of February saw sub-zero temperatures, and that
upon February 12th I climbed to a nest forty feet up in
an oak which held one egg upon which an owl stayed sitting until I was nearly to her level. . . . That the owlets
mature slowly and must have a long growing period to
reach full strength before Winter comes again, does not
satisfactorily explain it. Even in Florida where Winter
never comes, eggs are laid around Christmas. Moreover,
their cousin-species, Barred Owls, put off nesting a month
or more here, yet the offspring must lead just the same
kind of life.

Around mid-February also, the silvery notes of the
Chickadee begin to be heard with interspersings now and
then of its two-noted whistle. "Pheee-beee" sounds mellowly from the crusted woods on a sunny morning; rarely,
at first; then as days go by as common a call as one hears
until Robins come. And but let one sunny day arrive,
warmer than its predecessors, sap will start falling from
storm-broken twigs of the sugar maples. As if this were a
signal, as to a rendezvous out swarm the advance-guard
of little black sap-flies, having emerged from "eggs" in bark

crevices. Days may pass, Winter looks in again; every sap-
fly has disappeared, only to re-emerge if the thermostat in
their bodies reaches a certain temperature. Like three or
four species of spiders, they sleep lightly, and freezing
stiff means so little to them that almost any Winter thaw
starts them forth. Here Nature nods, "ababbling o' green
fields" in her sleep, betraying these petty mites of a day,
dooming them to even more abbreviated life than normally
they get. A thaw in these days is but a weak mirage of
Spring, not a prediction.— One might say too that some
other dwellers in the woods have had their sense of time
utterly confounded; skunk-cabbage and witch-hazel. The
one starts to bud in November, the other actually flowers
then, their seasons hopelessly muddled. Though the two
are in no manner harbingers of Spring, they do prophesy
it; certainly a cheering assurance in the year's *darkest*
hours. . . . Pussy-willow, now, there's a promise for you!
In no January which I can remember have I failed to provide my living room with vases of those buds, so stirringly
proclaiming from every soft tuft: "Be patient, Spring is on
the way!"

Willow twigs and those of red alder brighten with antici-
patory color along in February; the one markedly lighten-
ing its yellow, the other its ruby tints. Foxes, rabbits mate
under February's full moon.— Just what is it all these sensitive mechanisms hear or feel back there in mid-Winter:
willows, spiders, foxes, bunnies; that stirs them to activity?
Surely not transitory warmth alone; more likely they detect
the first faint increase in the count of ultraviolet getting
through to them from the rays of the lifting sun; the slight
lengthening of day. I noted that even on the Gulf Coast
where I stayed a short time last Winter, green things did
not bud very actively, nor birds think or sing of migration,
until sun warmth carried also that mystic radiation, —

THE FIRST WEEK OF MAY

which, of course, it does much earlier far to the south. . . .
March blows in. Red Squirrels "sing" and snicker more
excitedly, tap trees on their own account and drink the sap;
the Tree Sparrows from Athabaska and Hudson Bay, impatient to return, start practicing snatches of new song;
raccoons awake and prowl; skunk-cabbages go on with
their thrustings-up; moles tunnel out into the snow; soon
hepaticas start lifting liver-colored leaves off the forest
floor. . . . Then Spring *really arrives:* the first trill of the
Song Sparrow is heard in the land!

For me at least, that sound announces Spring; it is truly
news. Before bluebirds or robins return, this hardy, friendly
bird, numbers of which have fought the Winter through on
its own battleground, will greet the sunrise on a certain
early-March dawn with a tinkling, reedy rejoicing. My
misgivings are at rest — it *will* be Spring on the morrow.
And presently (often later on that very day), the robin and
bluebird will arrive, flocks of Rusty Blackbirds will hurry
by, Killdeers scream over and the Redwings come. These
six heard, Spring is established regardless of dates or
almanacs.

—About that petulant "first robin" controversy we go
through each April; truly, one robin does not make a Spring,
nor two or three; for, seemingly unrealized by writers-to-
the-editor and Press Service reporters, robins in small
groups often brave a northern Winter in sheltered spots,
then turn up themselves to enliven the argument.

After all, the four seasons, like the life of man, like the
epochs of history, do not start and stop, cease and begin;
they melt and merge into one another. Spring, one might
say, is where the heart is; a season which is as old as we
think it is. It begins when you want it to begin — and ends
when you cease to notice it.— Or as Thoreau put it:
"Spring.— March fans it, April christens it, and May puts

NOW THAT WE HAVE TO WALK

on its jacket and trousers. It never grows up, but drags its slow length along, ever springing, bud following close upon leaf — and when Winter comes it is not annihilated, but creeps on mole-like under the snow showing its face occasionally by fuming springs and watercourses. So let our manhood be . . . still advancing youth, bud following hard upon leaf. . . ."

Now, at long last, back to what does occur hereabout from May 1st to 8th: Ah, so much happens, or can happen! One's emotional tension accumulates with each day's experiences, developing into a constant state-of-expectancy, a hair-trigger alertness. Such brief slumber as in May I allot to the vegetative side of my own nature is grudged and regretted. Yet, I suppose, in a sense, "sleep is an opinion," as the French dramatic critic retorted when waked in the theatre. The six or seven hours forced on me actually are testimony as to what those days *mean*.

But for more concrete and particularized support beneath my statement that the aforesaid week is about high tide in the naturalist's year, I have looked through several years in my diaries, and, having concluded the period last May (1942) to be typical, and as interesting a week as these notes recall to mind, I am setting down — after some necessary editing — the record roughly as it stands. Be assured that more is left out than left in by the process.— That which appears in parenthesis is my present "editorial comment" or is inserted by way of elaboration.

May 1 — Friday

6 A.M. Five deer, including two yearlings, came from the woods, walked past the long woodpile, then filed through the vegetable garden to the road.

Hermit Thrushes *singing* while migrating past. Only

THE FIRST WEEK OF MAY

once before have I heard them here. Yes, the finest in bird music!

Found another spot along the upper brook where the Showy Orchis is just in bloom. That fragrance maybe one of the region's seven most superb odors.

The Dogwoods are just blanching into bloom — though it isn't blossoming. (The large white bracts back of the flower-head are what is generally called blossoms.)

While searching in Elmer's woods for the nest of that Great-horned Owl pair, came upon a Barred Owl nest which, climbing revealed, held three little fuzzy yellow infants. (In May nests of owls, hawks and crows are special objectives, for we bird-banders want to put identifying number-bands on the young.) On nest-rim lay decapitated bodies of a Star-nosed Mole, a Whitefoot Mouse and a Meadow Mouse. The open woods all around now show jack-in-pulpit, anemones, saxifrages, addertongue, mitrewort, bloodroot — and hepatica. One clump of birdfoot violet. (After one's sharp delight at finding hepaticas in bloom again, the old friend of childhood — of every country child, perhaps, — after waiting so long through a reluctant February and tantalizing March for the first sight; after a few days of seeing them spread everywhere *as though they were common-looking;* then; when you notice suddenly that the petals are falling, have all fallen; one feels a sinking of the heart like that which comes "While gazing on the happy Autumn fields and thinking of the days that are no more." — Alas, another Spring is going by; one more Spring already a part of yesterday! *It is always later than you think.*)

Saw the first Red Bat of the season at dusk. The (Louisiana) Water-thrush came from the Caribbean during last night, and sang loudly, constantly at six this morning along our brook. No bird except a wren sings as *many times* a season — what a boon of nature that a pair nests here by the brook year after year!

A large wave of Myrtle Warblers passed through, near-

[95]

ly all the males singing those quiet, *contented* short songs
of theirs. It was nearly dusk when I saw an elm full of
birds which at first I did not recognize. Studying them a
moment through the glasses, they were suddenly just
ordinary White-throats. In such an unexpected place! Determined shortly that they were all busily eating the nearly ripened elm seeds. Never heard or read of this before.
They are supposed to be always ground-feeders.

While we were eating lunch five loons went over halloo-
ing their loud but mellow calls that sounded tremulous
as if in eager anticipation of getting back to where water
could again be comfortably cool.

One of my hives acts as if it were preparing for swarming tomorrow.

May 2 — Saturday

Quite a stiff frost last night! But what a sunrise — over
sparkling frost, new leaves and birdsongs. Cucumber plants
in cold frame had their tips touched by the cold.

Cherry trees are in full bloom all about. — And today
"the" shadbush is full! (The full coverage of this particular tree down along the pasture fence, is an annual *event*
always to be noted down. The white blossoms burst in a
day, stay two, and scatter petals on the fourth. It can be
seen for miles. The event happens according to season,
all the way from April 20th to May 8th.)

The litter of three Gray Squirrels came out from their
hole in the lawn Black Walnut at daybreak and ran dutifully, steadily about for a half-hour. They appear to be
two-thirds grown already.

Heard the songs of two passing Solitary Vireos; there
is a resonant, bell-like, chiming quality to it which distinguishes it at once from that of all other vireos.

On a short walk through H's swampy woods this morning, we found an area of pink lady slipper carrying over
a hundred plants, in a dry spot we seemed to have over-

looked for years. (—One was a pure *white* flower, dazzling — and rare.) There's fragile beauty for you! Thoreau called them "all flower." The leaves do not rise much off the ground. — And *two* fat raccoons sleeping in an old crow's nest; sleeping, that *is*, until I pounded on the trunk of the hemlock; then they burst into life, shuffling like tiny bears around and around and up into comparative obscurity near the tree's tip. How droll their faces as they peer down! — Started a Red-tail Hawk from a nest along the further side of the swamp. Can't climb to it! Three young robins in the nest over the porch. Early birds.

My bees did swarm at noon. And they got away, mainly because they first landed in the climbing roses where I couldn't properly get at them.

Flock of Purple Finches singing in the elm while they ate seeds for an hour.

But the day's *feature* was the annual Goldfinch Chorus. For two solid hours some forty birds operated an uninterrupted *fountain of song* which flowed down from the burgeoning top of the elm — while they ate seeds, too. (When such a flock of Goldfinches come together in May, all singing at once, the effect is scintillant, like firework sparklers; no separate song can be distinguished; no break in the raining down of tinkling melody for hours on end. Perhaps this *is* the most spectacular bird music of all. It takes place in a period of only two or three days at most. At this Spring congregation of the small flocks of Wintertime, selection of partners is thought to take place. However, not for two months does nesting begin.)

Fringed polygala just starting to bloom. And the plant which bore *white* flowers last Spring carries them again this year.

Garden was plowed today. What a fascination there is about fresh and ready dirt — it looks *fecund*. Always, alas, more fecund that it proves. Strange how it yields squashes for a squash-seed and beans for a bean; side by side. Eight Red Crossbills eating oak-tassels — or insects on them(?).

[97]

NOW THAT WE HAVE TO WALK

Three large Rough-legged Hawks overhead — a *new* record for the species here. To date, list of birds seen carries fifty species.

Found two crow's nests each holding five eggs and one Red-shouldered Hawk's holding four. — Fodder for bird-banding next month.

A huge specimen of witch-hopple; a shrub we have never before found outside the Catskills and Adirondacks; came to light up in that little two-acre oasis of virgin hemlocks on Rocky Brook. Never suspected it until now! (The cathedral-aisle effects among these huge tree boles bring sharply back to me realization of what we all lost when, for tan-bark and stove-wood, men changed our great, vast forests into wood lots!) Witch-hopple is one of the most beautiful of our native shrubs when blooming.

Brought home in a quart jar several egg-masses each of Spotted Salamander and Wood Frog. Former has curved "larvae" in them about ready to emerge from the jelly. (—That little ice pond held about fifty egg masses. I practically never *see* one Salamander a year; yet on the first day after ice leaves this pond a *hundred* of them come together to mate and lay. Where *can* a hundred Spotted Salamanders live in that pasture! They are strictly nocturnal.)

May 4 — Monday

Apple blossoms are fully out now. And the big sugar maples are blossoming this year; a thing which occurs only once in two or three years. At this moment many of them near-by look almost like gigantic Forsythias, staggering under loads of yellow tassels. Leaves will come on shortly after this.

Four little chipmunks seen standing with their mother at the mouth of their burrow in the lawn. Three weeks old perhaps. Not half grown yet.

First Grouse nest 200 feet from the house; it holds twelve eggs.

THE FIRST WEEK OF MAY

All three, the painted, white and the red trilliums are now open in the woods.

Climbed to nest of a Cooper Hawk in hemlock which now holds three eggs. Saw two Broad-wing Hawks looking over the woods for a nesting site this morning.

A skunk at dusk walked leisurely from beneath the kitchen and started looking over the lawn for insect food. Most unusually, it allowed me to walk within six feet and stand talking to it, without being at all disturbed. We followed one another about for half an hour, both with a sense of mutual self-respect. It appeared to be exceedingly hungry. — Do you suppose there are *young* back there beneath the house.

The Bartramian (or Upland) Sandpipers are back! (There is a wide flat tract of wet low meadows a mile from home where three or four pairs of these highly interesting "shore" birds breed every year.)

May 5 — Tuesday

A whippoorwill whipped nearly all night. He'll be going on tomorrow though, they never take up residence here.

Yellow lady slippers which we transplanted last June to a damp spot in our woods are now out in full fragile beauty. Six of them.

Two Pileated Woodpeckers, huge, flashing creatures, appeared in the woods today, and seemed to be excavating either a roosting hole or a nesting hole in the top of a large maple. (They are fast getting commoner around here; used to be an almost legendary bird.)

While scything a plot alongside the garden, came upon another "rabbit's nest" deep in the clumps of orchardgrass. Could not be noticed, had I not lifted off a bit of the covering material with the scythe-tip. In it four very young bunnies — which alas, cannot grow up there and raid the garden two weeks from now.

[99]

NOW THAT WE HAVE TO WALK

Heard croaks of the Green Frogs just come to the pond to mate; next week will come the toads. Last week the last of the adult Wood Frogs left the water.

Came upon a Killdeer's nest on the moraine hog-back. Inside the eggs chicks could be heard faintly peeping.

A flock of some twenty brant went over the house before breakfast.

A lordly cock pheasant and three or four hens have established a series of nests in among my red pine plantation; almost stepped on a hen as she flew off from ten eggs beneath a small spruce, (and last week I found another nest with an egg in that vicinity.)

Leaves just starting to appear on butternuts and black walnuts. The red oak is in full bloom and the black oak too.

May 6 — Wednesday

Orioles arrived at dawn. . . And later we heard and saw a Cardinal. — Away up here from Dixie! Second record for all time. It was a male who did some minutes of whistling before we guessed what species it was; shortly after being seen, he disappeared. (And never was seen again!)

Leaves fast coming out to full size on maples and black cherry trees.

"Warbler Week" ended today. It is our biggest flight of warblers. Saw the *first* Worm-eating and Parulas. Total warbler species seen to date is twenty-four. (Rarest finds this year were the Kentucky and the Blue-winged Yellow.) The first Blackpoll Warbler shook its string of tiny bells over the lawn today. (These birds travel way up to northwestern Canada and into Alaska, and they get a very late start.)

At the edges of woodlands the Black Haw bushes stand out with their lavish displays of white, domed panicles. They are not common here. Puzzling at first to identify

[100]

them because they have the look of hawthornes, the leaves of the rose family, yet are among the honeysuckles. Grass sent jumping by night-before-last's rain. How vividly green the world is, whereas one month ago it still looked mostly yellow-and-brown!

May 7 — Thursday

Wild azalea, of which the back pastures have such a wealth, is just today starting to bloom. In fragrance and dainty loveliness, I think it not to be wondered at that Emerson penned his most lyrical poem when aroused by it.

("Rhodora! if the sages ask thee why
This charm is wasted on the earth and sky,
Tell them, dear, that if eyes were made for seeing,
Then Beauty is its own excuse for being: . . .")

And the white lilacs have come out. The whole yard is heavy with their odor.

The first hummingbird came to the columbines today. A male, of course; *she* will arrive ten days from now. — Just to think that since that pair went away last September, they have flown the Gulf of Mexico! Yet did not lose our address. They come back year after year.

The grouse nest behind the house found ravaged by crows — the eggs all smashed and eaten. (Records seem to prove that eight-tenths of *all* nests fail of final fruition.)

A *Western* Palm Warbler went through today; the first I ever identified; though we have numerous flights of the other Palm. It sang; no *Yellow* Palm ever sang for me in migration.

Climbed "The Mountain" today (elev. 1230') discovering the season to be about five days earlier than down here; yet but a half-hour is required to walk up.

Far Shall We Travel

Sweet is the scent of the dark loam
Fresh-furrowed on the hills of home;
Welcome the sting of autumn rain
And wind upon my face again;
Tender the sun, the feel of earth,
And after toil the firelit hearth.

But mellowed by the journeying years
Must I await the scythe or shears
And like the many-wintered tree
Ripen, fall and cease to be?
I'll face it now if this be so:
Ease your pack, my soul, and go! . . .

Far shall we travel, comrade, twinned
With viewless atoms on the wind,
Dissolve in rain, mix with dark earth
That brought the deathless gods to birth,
Survive such fire as Pelee pent
And thrive in every element.

—WILLIAM W. CHRISTMAN
Songs of The Western Gateway

CHAPTER VIII

THE LONGEST TRAIL IN THE WORLD

IN THESE days of asphalt, concrete and petroleum, where is the longest trail in the world? In Tibet? Mongolia? The Amazon Basin? Across the Great West? No, it lies along our eastern mountain-chain. Its name is the Appalachian Trail and it traverses the Appalachian System of highlands. Genghis Khan's great route, Pekin-to-the-Mediterranean; the Burma Road, Rangoon to Chunking; these were longer human *routes;* but the Longest Trail is by far the longest *trail,* and it is *marked* from end to end. It passes through a section of our country where automobile owners are most numerous and where, in general, the concrete road network has its smallest meshes. That Trail is 2050 miles long — yet is even *wider* than that, as we shall see — and it runs from Mount Katahdin, Maine, to Mt. Oglethorpe, Georgia. From mid-Maine to north-Georgia! It was finally completed, link to link, *only in 1937!*

An extraordinary trail and its creating a notable piece of human endeavor! Its very existence was comparatively unknown to the average American until quite recently; not only to those of our great majority whose footwork consists mainly in stepping on the gas; but to thousands who habitually spend days of joy-walking elsewhere in this widespread outdoors of ours, which is still one of America's proudest distinctions among nations.

A motorist would — or should — take at least eight days driving 2050 miles; the most fanatic devotee of hiking could not finish the long Long Trail in less than three months, if he died in the attempt. Only a handful of human beings have as yet covered its entire route; and these few

did so by annually taking it section by section over a stretch
of several years. . . .

At first thought it seems a sheer anachronism that the lonely Appalachian Trail should develop in these times when
every possible inducement is being made to keep Americans
spending money and staying close to places where money
could fastest be spent. — It is rendered plausible only when
one reflects that a deep, quiet current of nature appreciation, a persistent yearning for escape from cities, is alive
among us and has been one of the factors helping quietly,
steadily to create our new federal forests and parks, state
parks and private wild preserves uncountable. This yearning, plus a countrywide acknowledgment of the *economic
importance of conservation* in all its aspects, have played
major parts in the movement. Surely our descendants will
bless us for this great conservation policy — now but some
thirty years old.

The spiritual start of the Trail goes back about twenty-
two years; the idea was largely of one man's launching.—
Like many another humane institution, the tangible result
today is but "the lengthened shadow of one man." In 1921
a certain outdoor enthusiast and author, Benton MacKaye,
conceived and proposed the idea as "A Project in Regional
Planning." A year or so later the new Appalachian Trail
Club (shortly after developing into the present A. T. Conference) and the United States Forestry Service started
to work in earnest building the dream-trail. When this task
began there were of course many miles of woodland ribbons
along the Appalachians. Some were ancient Indian and
pioneer paths. To piece together the numerous ribbons and
to thread one continuous line through the several wild
playgrounds of the East was a breath-taking vision. Today,
behind its completion lie years of propaganda and organization, not to mention sessions of legislatures, conferences of

officials, and miles of hard labor in the wilderness. Ideas such as this do not take fire with a single match.

No less than forty-two constituent outdoor organizations, representing in 1928 over 10,000 members, joined themselves in that year into a more vigorous and permanent body: the Conference. By now this centralized body (divided into six sectional conferences) whose activities are *entirely voluntary* and who *employ no salaried employees,* represents many times that number of citizen supporters. Its "coefficient of expansion" in future has no mathematical limits. Every indication is that this "body" is not yet grown up to full stature; and eventually, for all we know, the audacious Trail may yet be pushed to Labrador — and perchance to Hudson Bay!

The Trail direction is generally southwest-northeast. It is intended to follow where possible the *crest* of the ranges of the eastern Appalachian chain. By reason of the diverse mountain structure along its northern sections, its route is decidedly irregular, alternating the ascents of peaks and the crossings of valleys. For the most part it leads through a wilderness area, though by necessity it passes in some regions through farming communities and a few towns. So it varies greatly in character. In some few areas it is extremely rough and difficult, scarcely showing any improvement work on the footway whose routing is indicated almost wholly by the A. T. markers on trees; while in other sections, as if to make up, it becomes a graded *path* — but not for long. Most of the long stretch is no high-heeler's way, no silk-stocking promenade. It is woodland and mountain trail such as even Dan'l Boone might not scorn — though doubtless he would find paint-and-metal markings unnecessary, preferring axed tree-blazes instead. It climbs and climbs in some places, in others it drops and drops. Yet, all in all, it is a modernized route — that is, in the sense

[*105*]

of being a *marked* and regularly traveled route, in some extensive sections having lean-tos and other shelters spaced regularly for walkers' use.

Obviously, *just walking along a path* is not all there is to an extended outdoor tramp. One must eat day after day — and how one does eat, this author knows well from many days of experience — but not as Boone's kind did, by rifle and fish-hook. Modern pioneers can but rarely do without an occasional night's sleep under a roof sure not to leak on a bed which is not thereby soaked and sodden. Furthermore, appropriate supplies and medical service become necessary once in a while. Therefore, the skyline trail for the most part, while intentionally avoiding, wherever it can, civilization's conveniences and annoyances, is at only few places far removed from civilization's first aids. Likewise, log or plank shelters dot the dotted-line of the route; they are multiplying like mushrooms after a Summer rain; any total given out today would be an out-dated figure six months hence.— The Trail Conference publishes a corrected list every January which can be relied upon confidently.

Walkers on the Trail from end to end — and, as I said, such beings actually exist — can touch the soil of fourteen States. Were such a hiker to stay on the main, officially marked path, he would traverse two or three National Parks and eight National Forests. If he but diverge a bit here and there upon connecting trails, he might visit three or four more federal Forests and many State-owned preserves. Not only may such major parks and forests be reached through branching trails, but by means of hundreds of other connecting roads and trails, a practically *endless* exploration of contiguous countryside could, year after year, be made. It was estimated in 1935 that no less than 2500 miles of additional trailage connected. So *wide*, therefore, is the way, that actually *no man knoweth* the width of its influ-

[*106*]

ence and scope. The green Catskills and the greener and longer Green Mountains of Vermont are but a few steps off the main right-of-way, as indeed are the Adirondacks.

By any yardstick, by any scale for estimating human endeavor, this great trail is an important achievement of democracy. It is truly a chapter or epoch of the American Dream. A "labor of love" in large measure, it is a memento of one of our countrymen's most unselfish inspirations. Its organization and upkeep has demanded no end of planning and hard work yielding no thought of monetary return. Americans working together, that is what made it. If we can today use honestly the slogan: "Civilian Defense — that is You!" likewise accurately could it be said: "The Trail — it is You!" for its inception and most of its construction came out of citizen cooperation and grass-roots enthusiasm. . . .

Let us get back on the Trail.— This is the route of it: Beginning in Georgia's section of the Chattahoochee National Forest, at a point on Mt. Oglethorpe where stands a white marble shaft commemorating the State's founder, it goes into Blue Ridge country and into Tennessee; next strikes the Nantahala Forest. On summits it traverses the Great Smokies and Pisgah Forest and Unaka Forest and Cherokee Forest — areas almost too huge for a Northeasterner's mind to grasp! Two days' walk further it enters Natural Bridge Park in the Old Dominion State, the State wherein lies *one-fourth of the whole Trail,* then on through George Washington Forest into Shenandoah National Park. Presently the traveler reaches historic Harpers Ferry where is "the only movable part of the Trail" (as someone remarked); there he takes a boat over into Maryland. Soon the way leads through the Gettysburg Battleground. After Gettysburg, the trail passes almost straight up the rough stretches of the Alleghenies which, in baffling parallel ridges, occupy a third of Pennsylvania; that mountain

wilderness which for so many years proved an effective
dam against the stream of settlement into the Ohio Country
behind. Here it crosses the Susquehanna near Harrisburg
and leaves the State at Delaware Water Gap, passing then
up along the Kittatinny Range in New Jersey; next rides
the Poconos and enters Bear Mountain Interstate Park
along the Hudson. Now across the long Bear Mountain
Bridge into the rugged terrain along the New York-Connec-
ticut line. Presently it threads the Berkshires and starts
into Vermont, there using the route of the older Long Trail
in that State, to a point below Killington High Peak. Here
the route leaves the Long Trail, turns east, does brief
justice to the White Mountain country, and ends (after 266
miles) by crossing Maine to its highest point, Mt. Katahdin.

The public domain which this trail either crosses or gives
indirect access to is nearly half a billion acres! You could
lose the whole Balkans in it! It contains some of the grandest
and most diversified scenery on earth. If every soul in the
United States stood in single file on these many trails the
queue would not fill them. The writer never has found
them crowded. How could they be crowded? Indeed, now
and then, he has run across a wayfarer who mildly com-
plained of the loneliness. . . .

Surely in this new golden age of hiking is a partial solution to that "leisure time problem" of which we now hear
so much. There is no problem. There is only lack of imagination — or lack of gumption. This trail, this mammoth
amateur recreational project, dwarfs any in the world.
Our children's and children's children's hobby and health
ambitions are largely taken care of by it — on it. Nearly
every kind of animal, bird, insect, plant, tree and mineral
in the East may be searched for along the great trail.
Whether one walks on it six miles or sixty, or even spends
a hasty Sunday, he can have of Nature about what he

wants.— Some section or other of the trail lies within one hour by motor from half the people in the United States. How many eastern Americans realize that! . . .

Is there not irresistible lure and romance in these names: Shenandoah, Cherokee, the Great Smokies, Mammoth Cave, Mount Mitchell (highest point east of the Mississippi; it is crossed by the trail), Kittatinny, Tuckerman's Ravine? Historical lore oozes from each. Who is there that reads about "stands of virgin timber," "unspoiled waterfalls," "silent, wilderness-bounded lakes," who will not call those pioneer trailmen blessed, and go forth to behold these things? Here is what the Forest Service itself thinks it means by its part in opening the Long Trail and the others into our public domains: "The National Forests of the East and South are protecting the watersheds and helping control the flow of the most important rivers and streams; they are producing continuous timber crops; they are demonstrating to the public the technique and results of extensive practical forestry; they are great, free public playgrounds, and they are furnishing homes and protection to game animals, birds and fish." And this is what Mr. Benton MacKaye meant, and foresaw, even prior to the Forest Service's truly practical treatment of that wilderness: "The pioneer opened through a forest a path for the spread of civilization. His work was nobly done and the life of the town and city is in consequence well upon the map in our country. Now comes the great task of holding this life in check — for it is just as bad to have too much urbanization as too little. America needs her forests and her wild, open spaces quite as much as her cities and her settled places." . . .

Well . . . there is now, in reality, "a long, long trail awinding into the land of our dreams." It is for all of us. It is ours. We own it.

NOW THAT WE HAVE TO WALK

For any of my readers who feel the urge to use the trail and to have part in its upkeep and protection, communicating with the Appalachian Trail Conference will open that opportunity to them. There is a unit-organization of the Conference in their locality which they may join, and local clubs all along the Trail. . . .

* * *

It was related that John Randolph of well-known colonial memory, once spent a night upon the summit of one of the pinnacled Peaks of Otter. (— Could he have imagined *possibly* that a century and a half later Long Trail walkers would take leave of a Natural Bridge National Park over these remote peaks!) He was accompanied only by a faithful black servant. When day broke and the sun rose upon a scene of wild misty splendor, he was so moved that, turning to his humble companion, with a choke he said: "Never from this hour believe anyone who tells you there is no God!" Now, today, any one of us standing as he stood, upon one of a hundred peaks, Maine to Georgia, can exclaim aloud or to himself: "No longer is there any doubt but that this is the most wonderful trail in the world! . . . And it really and truly *exists!*"

Will its upkeep and its protection and the glory and beauty of its surroundings prove to be a heavier load than democracy can bear? The growing use of it poses a few serious doubts. Will its shelters and their facilities be treated with mature consideration? Will vandalism increase upon public land as it can upon private lands not patrolled? One half its mileage runs across private holdings, and private interests at any time may demand its relocation, if they are forced into such a dilemma.— Most particularly, will there come forth from future ranks of democracy the kind of human enthusiasm which built the Longest Trail

THE LONGEST TRAIL IN THE WORLD
on earth? Will its upkeep be neglected? The torch is being
handed on, right at this moment of time, for the pioneers
of this dream, the prime-movers from 1921 to 1943, are
passing — along a still longer trail which, alas, does not
end in Georgia or in Maine. . . .

The Appalachian Trail Conference publishes several
pamphlets (as well as guide-books and maps) which the
trail hiker — on any trail — will find full of valuable information upon outfit, clothing, season, foods, etc. Send a
stamp for its list of publications. — 808 Seventeenth St.
Washington, D. C.

As the marsh-hen secretly builds on the watery sod,
Behold I will build me a nest on the greatness of God:
I will fly in the greatness of God as the marsh-hen flies
In the freedom that fills all the space 'twixt the marsh and
　　the skies:
By so many roots as the marsh-grass sends in the sod
I will heartily lay me a-hold on the greatness of God. . .

　　　　　　—SIDNEY LANIER: *The Marshes of Glynn*

CHAPTER IX

KNEE-DEEP IN MARSH

WHAT a place to walk! The boggy, muddy, reedy, bushy, bubbling swamp. Treacherous, quaking waste foresworn by man; infested by reptiles, spiders, snails; by unknown terrors; crawling things, darting, stinging things; ill-smelling, trackless, lonely, loathsome, stagnant, slimy!

Is that what you think it is? Many otherwise venturesome and dynamic individuals do shrink from going down to the marsh in boots with a spiritual squeamishness not unlike that which the Mediterranean world once felt about venturing into the sea beyond the Pillars of Hercules. Very, very few "normal" people go wading around in such places; it seems so footless a thing to do.

But what awaits you there? Well, suppose you draw on a spare pair of hip-boots and come along. We shall see what we shall see — and may lay those moldy ghosts of apprehension forever. . . . It is May 30th. We have almost reached Thornton's Swamp, you and I; we have resolved to take all sights and sounds yonder to be our province. We can say we intend to search again for "that Marsh Hawk's nest" to get some better and more candid photographs. Thus equipped, with a normal reason; thus properly excused from duty, we shall be sure of conscience-free leisure; and whatever else befalls us will be grist for our mill; top-cream on the milk of a perfect May day. . . .

Hank Thornton is hoeing-out hills for corn planting as we pass along his land. "Goin' sucker fishin'?"

"Nope."

Glancing at our hip-boots: "Trapin' mushrats?"

"Nope."

NOW THAT WE HAVE TO WALK
" 'Sright, too late fer that. . . . Froggin'?"

"Nope."

"Catchin' turtles?"

"Nope."

He gives it up in obvious disapproval, mystified; resumes his hoeing; and we go on down the lane, disappear from his sight around a bend, cross a stone wall, start up a slight rise. . . Yes, it is a more delicate mission we are on than a Thornton could have guessed. The fact is that we are on our way to this sixty-acre swamp because — we *have* to go! Is it chiefly to locate that hawk's nest? — We will be frank, and now we are so far from home and so near the swamp, we will answer, "No!" The objective is not by any means only that two-by-two-feet homestead among the wildrose bushes, sweet-flag and sphagnum. The success of the trip cannot be measured by the scant fortuity of finding something tangible to fetch home — or even to report. It will matter little what our hands bear at the end of this expedition. For, as Moslems make holy pilgrimages, as the Sock-eye Salmon migrate through the incredible miles of the north Pacific, as the Golden Plover visits the two antipodes; so, to us there come now and again through the year these savage urges to go, go — "something hidden, go and find it!" To a mountain top; to a glen; to a dim hemlock forest on a hillside. Then, there comes one Spring day when we, too, like the lowly Spadefoot Toad, are resurrected by a secret signal and betake ourselves to the teeming marsh. A curious passion absorbs us, for living among the marsh creatures for a moment, watching them, feeling a little with them; seeing, finding, perhaps something different from anything we found before. . . .

Surely there is more *life* per unit of volume in marsh air, water and mud, than in any other earthly medium — even despite man's fecund success in crowding himself into cities. Whether we look at its water and mud through a microscope, or view it as landscape, or see it with a naturalist's or a hunter's eye, how teeming the marsh is with a various and illimitable vitality! In its stagnant water lives, and has lived since time immemorial, that tiny one-celled microcosm named Paramecium, whose reproduction is accomplished — simply by splitting itself into two Paramecia, a process called by biologists "fission." Its reproducing faculty can roughly be indicated by a momentary flashback into our algebra book. The formula for the sum of a geometrically increasing series of numbers ("fissions") is:

$$\text{Sum} = \frac{A(R^n - 1)}{R - 1}$$

If A be taken as your first Paramecium; 'n' the number of fissions; 'R' the redoubling each time; that is, 2; then, what do we find is the result in *five years* if a Paramecium "reproduces" fourteen times a week? In plain English it means the number of individuals resulting could be so great (if all survived) that "the mass would fill our universe to the limits of the Milky Way." — Ah, but of course death must match life, in the long run, in every species under the sun; or else life itself simply could not continue. — Which is the esoteric truism beneath all two-faced gods; beneath Shiva and Parvati; Zarathustra and Ahriman; Satan and Christ.

Why should the marsh not teem? It is the ancient matrix out of which, through the ages, have come all the beasts of the field and fowls of the air, and man himself. Marshes, the geologist tells us, are dead or dying lakes; lakes, where they are not of the recent, glacial-dug kind, are miniature counterparts of the vast shallow seas of the long Paleozoic and Mesozoic wherein all previous life was reshaped. The lakes of the world are all temporary — a little more temporary than the everlasting hills — all lakes are slowly being filled up; to marsh and at last to land. All marshes are moribund too. Marsh life is oldest of all in lineage; most all the stratified, sedimentary rocks on earth were laid down in such places. And today the life they retain is concentrated, crowded, highly specialized for persistence. The magic pitcher of the world is still exhaustless where a swamp persists. In a swamp life is very real; subsistence, struggle, reproduction, defense, disaster, delight, all have settings in its fastnesses. A state of nature yet prevails there richer, more varied, more undisturbed by surrounding human occupation, than in any of the other land "biologic zones," except perhaps the lone tundra wildernesses. . . .

As we ascend the rise of ground overlooking Thornton's Swamp we hear deep beyond in the marsh a snatch of avian rag-time, Chunk-ala-plunk which seems to boil up from under water. The Bittern is the first swamp denizen we hear. But first by only a moment, for with a squawk, a Green Heron leaves the near-by margin to flap across to a lonely clump of willows out in the wavering waste. Upon alighting he stands at such stiff attention that, if we take our eyes from him a second, we cannot detect him. We descend. Two or three Wood Turtles, started from toadstool meals beneath the sweet-fern, clumsily pretend to be furtive and still. Into the mud-and-water shallows we step — at last ankle-deep in marsh.

A school of half-developed tadpoles, haunting the shallows to evade certain cannibalistic traits in their elders, start zigzagging muddily down into deeper water. These are of course last season's tadpoles of Bullfrog and Green Frog, which require two Summers for maturing. We begin to note many long-laid egg-masses of frog and Spotted Salamander eggs clustered among the water-plants; gelatinous nebulae full of tiny nucleated spheres which, by as wonderful a process as that by which worlds are made, will

soon be backboned batrachians. — Yet, after all, nothing is
more wonderful than anything else — no matter where you
encounter it! The efforts of all those adult frogs to efface
themselves from our invading steps are strikingly un-
maternal and unpaternal. Like the so-called "gender" of
French and German nouns, frog-gender is by this date a
merely nominal distinction. Few creatures in the vertebrate
ranks show less sex-distinction eleven-twelfths of the year.
After May is gone; even after April has ended, with some
species; romance goes out of their lives entirely.

Dragon-fly and Damsel-fly volplane, rise and make perfect six-point landings everywhere about us — perhaps you
had not noticed how in flight they resemble miniature
monoplanes. As we step deeper and deeper; to our calves,
to our thighs, marsh gas bubbles up at every step — but
no Marsh Hawks appear. Overhead while we have been
wading are flying a score of Redwings in great parental
anxiety. Their nests, some with partly completed clutches
of scrolled-and-etched eggs of French-blue; some only at
the scaffolding-stage of construction; are appearing fre-
quently, right under our noses. Now we begin to balance
from clump to clump on the tussock-grass which we have
mounted as the water deepened; these often lurch off side-
ways or sink slowly under our weight. This balancing is
delicate work; hot work; though we have not yet reached
the section of cattail and flag towards which we are bound.

"There she goes!" — And there she does go — but with a
croak. Not a Marsh Hawk, a Bittern rises and flaps over the
bushes. We wade to the spot. A high and dry flat nest on a
tussock holds five odd-colored eggs as large as a Leghorn's.— Colored, I would say like "an olive starting to turn
brown;" for it is apter description than that "Isabella-
brown" color often used in books; an odd sort of designation
—which has even more oddly descended to us from the

[*117*]

tale of the Spanish Princess who wore, as a vow, her chemise many, many weeks — in fact over three years! —We see here that this curious shade has a great protective value; the eggs are unlikely to be conspicuous to crows, jays and other potential marauders flying above. . .

—"And, look, there's the hawk!"— Now flitting nervously overhead, occasionally tumbling characteristically about like an awkward moth — where has she risen from? The location of that often sought spot is as mysterious as ever. At a "chack, chack" from the opposite direction, we turn to confront the masculine member. Is there here not a clear case of miscegenation? When together they seem to be of two species; the female larger, browner. The tumbling, falling antics make evident the reason they were Latinized under the name Circus by the Namer-of-Names — himself nameless. Watching, we have remained quiet so many minutes that our presence is being forgotten. A faint splashing off to the left. A Muskrat swims across a space of open water making for his Winter home yonder, a large mound of sticks and flagstems roofed with thatch, which has carried him and his through the cold as snug and dry as a water-rat could desire. Several other lodges are in sight. Within a rod of its mound the rat dives and a row of bubbles marks the way to his underwater door. We wade over. Since he has made a deep furrow in the mud leading to the entrance, we avoid the trail. But I overlook a side entrance. With a quick slide both feet find it; the water merrily gurgles over the tops of my boots. Scrambling, falling forward, I draw myself up on the muskrat house on hands and knees, and lifting one leg after the other pour out of the boots all the water I can. In the sky overhead the chacking of the hawks sounds irritatingly exultant. The lodge quivers with my exertions until it seems certain that any occupants have fled. I tear off the top of the

rounded pile to show you what a snug home it is and we
peer into the grass-lined chamber beneath. — We are smit-
ten by remorse: here one conservative rat family has not
gone into Summer quarters in a hole in the bank, but has
decided to stay out here in mid-marsh! Shrinking back
into one angle, her shiny, beady eyes looking straight into
ours, is mother-rat. From beneath her peep a tiny twitching
nose and two small pink tails. Her own rich fur glints like
sealskin in the dim interior which exhales strongly that not
indelicate odor of her race. As desperate as a lion at bay,
she has scorned escape because her babies could not follow
her safely down through the trap-door into deep water. We
are a new kind of enemy. Except the Horned Owl at night,
the only natural foe this animal need fear is the water-
snake. What writhing, gripping battles must at times be
fought in the darkness of these nests!

I interlace some cut-off alder branches over the cavity
and replace the thatching. High above gyrate the hawks;
it is a sort of circus-day for us all. Now you and I begin our
search; plotting off the expanse of the wide marsh, we plod
up and down in parallel courses a quarter of a mile long.
Occasionally the hawks scold; at times dally indifferently
in a far end of the marsh as if frog-hunting, and are un-
concerned with the foolish crawling bipeds below. It is
all play-acting. . . Up and down we plod, slip, slide and
plunge under the lusty sun. Here an awakened snake nearly
as large as a man's wrist whips off from a mat of weeds with
a rasping of scales; there a Sora Rail or a Virginia Rail
flutters over the cattails, legs dangling, or they dart mouse-
like into the shadows ahead of us. We hear in the distance
the startled cry of some frog seized from the depths and
dragged thither by snapper or snake. — How it pulsates,
this marsh life; it is a stern race for a place in the sun — for
an hour!

[*119*]

NOW THAT WE HAVE TO WALK

We sit for a time on a huge boulder in mid-marsh. On the far-off hillside there is Hank Thornton stooping along in the sun making mechanical motions with a soundless hoe. . . . As if in gentle protest against all this disturbance down in the wastes, a Mourning Dove in the bordering thicket sobs, "OHHH! oh . . . oh . . . oh," in fading cadence.— May at high-noon.

A May-fly larva laboriously ascends a cattail stalk beside us; pauses a moment,— then walks right out of its skin! Leaving the translucent husk a perfect mummied replica behind, she dances now a new birth in the sun. A Fly-killer cruises by, snatches a luckless Bluebottle on the wing and settles to devour it. A Painted Turtle, then a Musk, poke up inquiring beaks to see if the basking-rock is still usurped. A sinister Snapper crawls past along the bottom mud seeking something, anything living, to clamp its jaws upon. . . . All at once we are aware of a queer ventriloquistic, quivering, mellow whistle dropping down from the zenith; a faint opening quaver, then long-drawn-out crescendo-diminuendo; seeming to inhale-exhale a breath, a sigh. It is like the earth swaying with a rhythm, uneasy of the abundance it holds and must soon outpour. . . . Where? And where again? — Oh, far above, three circling Upland Plovers; members of the little colony Thornton's old pasture has been host to these many seasons.— Ventriloquism with wings. . . .

With a start we rub our dozing eyes! — Mrs. Circus Hudsonius has just dived straight down and out of sight. We wait for her reappearance, frog or snake in her talons. But she does not come. We splash directly to the spot. This time she butterflies gracefully up from amid a clump of alders we thought we had looked into. Six inches from the moist sphagnum floor she and her mate have built a structure of twigs and cattail stalks, and lined it with dried grasses. It holds four faintly bluish eggs, of a size a Bantam would be proud to lay. A few tufts of downy brown feathers cling to the twigs roundabout. The sitting hawks; both of whom are known to brood; to while away the hours of incubation, have hacked at the surrounding alders with their sharp beaks. Their appeals now become piteous that we spare this their treasure; the previous chacking quite changes and they fly close to our heads. . . . Photography dutifully accomplished we leave . . .

Next to the south end of the marsh to learn whether the Arethusa and the Calopogon orchids are yet beginning to bloom in the cranberry bog.— Buds, but no blooms. . . . The watchful Upland Plovers still mellowly call down from the sky, but seem to wish to come no nearer. A pair of King-fishers is digging out a hole in the sand bluff along the stream which drains the swamp; a Killdeer starts worrying ahead for fear we might come ashore and flush its mate brooding out there in the meadow. We have no such inten-tion. We have our collecting bottles to fill with the different kinds of belated frog and salamander egg-masses we can find. And with *strings* of toad eggs, for that is the odd variation the toad originates among all the amphibians. There are submerged insect larvae to collect also, and a new water weed we had never before seen. The flotsam and the jetsam of the immemorial ooze from here and there on the bottom, we pick up too. We shall go over it later under the lens and microscope. . . . At length we drag weary, waterlogged feet homeward, to the final relief of hawks and redwings. . . . We have waded a marsh together, you and I; we shall be friends forever!

[*121*]

To me every hour of the light and dark is a miracle,
Every cubic inch of space is a miracle,
Every square yard of the surface of the earth is spread
    with the same,
Every foot of the interior swarms with the same. . . .

Why, who makes much of a miracle ?
As to me I know of nothing else but miracles. . . .

—WALT WHITMAN: in "Miracles": Leaves of Grass

CHAPTER X

OWLS ARE DIFFERENT

I BELIEVE that few amateur ornithologists — or call them bird lovers or bird hobbyists — few Americans interested in birds know much of anything about owls *at first hand;* probably comparatively few have so much as seen a wild one of any species. I hazard this sweeping generalization with confidence partly because I can so well remember that in my early teens (— and I was one of the rabidist of birders in those days!) I had had so few sights of them that I held them to be exceedingly rare, inhabiters, most of them, of far-off wilderness areas; and being haunters of night, never could be seen anyway; for me little or nothing was to be known about them. (— As is the widespread feeling about bats.) At any rate, nowadays I meet few nature enthusiasts in whose experience owls are not more or less a legend or a myth.

To the non-professional Audubonist, then, the owl clan are always "out there," a standing challenge, a baffling Northwest Passage, a mocking frontier beyond his hobbyland, ever receding, ever affording that sense of dissatisfaction in tallies and achievements so requisite for keeping any hobby alive with urgent, goading vitality.

Fortune has smiled in my later relations with them; I have written a good many words about owls and owls in my life; in all my books there are chapters on them.[1] Now, just here, I am merely setting down what I conceive to be the "essence," so to speak, of that odd category Owl-

[1] See the Author's *Walk, Look & Listen*, p. 5, and *Doorway To Nature*, p. 191.

dom, with the notion that walkers and birders everywhere might be both reminded and reassured; that they really can go forth and do something about making owl acquaintanceships. It is not too difficult; it is worth the effort. While owls are *not* common, and not easy to sleuth down, they are not nearly as rare as is generally supposed. Yet truly they comprise a group apart from the usual run of bird life; in a number of ways they are — different.

Living furtively, secretly, seldom seen by day, there are some ten species of owls reasonably numerous — not meaning abundant — in Canada and United States. Standard reference books will give you their ranges and living habitats. America has woodland owls, deep forest owls, marsh owls, desert owls, tundra or Arctic owls, barn owls; large owls, and those not so large.— Those which nest in tree crotches, in barn lofts and steeples, in ground burrows, in tree cavities. A wide gamut of choice open to you; a species to challenge every variety of staminas and skills. Differing widely among themselves in some minor particulars, in size, habitat and markings, yet they differ most particularly from all other bird groups. We might have thought of them — a few years back — as an Aryan race amongst the world's feathered tribes; so hardy and tough are they, so militant their habits; they are "a race apart" if any bird race is. In no less than ten particulars owls as a group or Family (Strigidae) are unique.

But, one moment! Have *you* ever seen a wild owl? . . . Winter and very early Spring is the time for seeking them. If you are at long, long last to identify some of these ten mysterious strangers by sight, it goes without saying you would have to do some "homework" in books to get the lay of the land they inhabit, learn their size and markings. When leaves are off and a living is harder to make in ice and snow, then owl tactics are bolder in hunting and mating

[*124*]

than when they resort to the canny secretiveness characteristic of their nesting days. On a cold quiet evening under
the stars of January and February the calls of some species
will carry as far as three miles. Such calls are valuable clues
for you to follow since as a rule the birds remain pretty
closely to one spot all the year. . . .

Those ten particulars. Well, first, so far as I am aware
none of our American owls are protected by law. They
enjoy no closed season. They are beyond the law; they are
outlaws. Every man's hand may be raised against them —
and there is no recourse. A strangely vindictive attitude
for these modern days of science — when, in fact, it is positively known that all species have their place in the scheme
of things and that no vital brick may be removed from the
wall-of-life without weakening, altering the structure —
when it is known that even an owl has his ecological purposes, his vital role that he has played since before mankind
was a primate. The majority of citizens owning shotguns,
influenced by a long handed-down tradition, regard all
owls as deserving the death penalty on sight, without benefit of *habeas corpus;* as vermin, pests, like "snakes designed
by the Creator to be enemies of men," of his game and his
poultry. And two other probable reasons exist for this
aggressive warfare against them; the one clearly obvious,
the second less so. First, the members of this persecuted
race are all predators, meat eaters, wild hunters competitive
with human gun-toters. They are called "rapacious" and
"raptorial" birds — even by the word-conscious scientists,
and inasmuch as hunters-with-shotguns are also rapacious
and raptorial to a marked degree; whether or not they
acknowledge it — they do not take kindly to that trait in
others. Wars between men being invariably referred to as
"defensive" by both sides, so, quite as logically, man's warfare against nature is not regarded as aggressive but merely

[*125*]

as retaliatory and protective.— An easy rationalization which does not need to be based upon facts. And is not. For modern research has determined that we have been mostly mistaken as to the predominance of game and poultry in raptorial diet. It has proved that we may not upset the balance of nature without most unforeseen repercussions.— Darwin a century ago, remember, showed by his classic cat-field mouse-bumblebee-clover study that large hay crops in England and house-cat scarcity were directly connected. When hawks and owls are decimated by shooting, their natural prey of mice, weasels, rats, gophers, skunks, do more devious damage in the long run than ever the birds do. . . . The other reason for anti-owl prejudice is very likely that most of us rarely meeting owls at all believe about everything we hear concerning their predacious habits. We know in general little about owl traits or food; if we did, is it not likely we would become interested in protecting them as we do other birds? — The French saying goes: "to know all is to forgive all."

Besides the two characteristics above mentioned: their legal status and their diet, the owl Family is unique in eight other particulars. And this uniqueness has singularly few exceptions. Moreover, few if any birds in other Families exhibit traits specifically owlish; few if any owls are there which do not fall into line with all eight of the following generalizations:

Owls are nocturnal; they detect prey by hearing not by sight; they do not regularly migrate, being resident in a given locality the year around; the wings of owls are shod with down, *i. e.* along the feather-edges, so that the birds fly and pounce noiselessly; they speak in voices weird and lugubrious; they practically never construct nests, using those made and abandoned by other birds or animals; owls nest very early in the year; they swallow their prey whole

OWLS ARE DIFFERENT

or in large fragments and after digestion *regurgitate* the fur, feathers and bones in pellets.

Can owls see in the dark? Are they blind in daylight? At first thought it would seem as if they must see well at night to locate little skulking creatures and to dodge branches; but when you realize what an amazing ear they have, a sense of hearing truly astonishing, a power of super-sight is not called for. To credit that keenness fully you must see it operate. I recall a Barn Owl of my youthful days who resided in our huge hayloft, a hide-out dark as a pocket after sundown. We could tell from hearing their squeaks that it often caught mice up there in the blackness. By the following Spring not a mouse apparently remained. . . . One Autumn evening, crouched among some clustered hemlock saplings I was listening to a Screech Owl "sing." A hundred feet distant, it was silhouetted against a faintly moonlit sky. Suddenly near me a tiny bird stirred ever so slightly on its hidden perch. The Screecher set itself, launched straight to the hemlock cover, picked off that luckless victim with scarcely a pause in the swoop and flew off noiselessly into the shadows.

It is obvious to anyone who has disturbed owls in the day-time that they can see to fly through the trees quite as readily as we could if we had wings.

No, neither blindness by day nor sight by night "explains" these things; but the gift of widening and shutting, in a broad range, the pupil-opening enables an owl's eye (like a cat's) to catch all the light there is at night and to avoid the comparative glare of day. It is well known by those who have practiced doing it, that even in darkest nights we actually can see well enough to walk through fairly open terrain. An owl's comparatively larger pupil admits more of this diffused illumination than does our own. . . .

An apparent exception to the non-migratory generalization about owls is the fact that the large Snowy Owl of the Canadian tundras is not infrequently seen in Winter throughout the northern States. In some years greater numbers come than in others; a sort of regularly recurrent cycle of rarity and commonness has been established — a fact governing a few other kinds of Canadian birds also. Up until recently it was accepted that these northerners came because of a corresponding cycle of *food-shortages* in the wilds. But a recent study (reported in *The Auk,* Oct. 1939) appears to upset the idea. A large fraction of these "migrants" are found to be juveniles. The theory reached is to the effect that because of *unusually favorable food supply* during the previous Summer or two, successful rearing of larger owl families has resulted. This surplus of birds accounts for the southward dispersal; not that the current Winter hardships force the species down here, as has been supposed. The cycle of greatest numbers in the United States comes a year or two after peaks of food-plenty up in the North; not in periods of food-scarcity. Obviously, this kind of occasional wandering of younger birds is not true seasonal migration at all.

As for that owl trait of early nesting, I can report several ascents in frigid and early February to Great Horned Owl nests wherein eggs lay circled by outer ice-fringes, the nest's center being kept open clear of snow by the sitter's body; the snow beyond being partly melted into ice by its body-warmth. My notebooks hold several records of Great Horns known to have laid eggs during periods of zero weather, or just after. For example in 1934. It was a very severe Winter all over the Northeast; therefore it may not be necessary to say that where I live in the Catskill Foothills the month of February set an all-time record for bitter cold. Yet upon February 18 — in the middle of that month of zero nights and near-zero days — I found a Great

[*128*]

OWLS ARE DIFFERENT

Horn brooding a large round billiard ball of an egg in a shallow, unlined nest of sticks situated in a crotch of a tall, wind-swept oak. Three days later, a second climbing revealed that she had laid another egg and, her normal clutch thus completed, was starting her four weeks' stint of incubation.[2] In the three day interval heavy snow fell, and one night recorded ten below zero at my home. My second visit saw the rim of the nest circled by lacy ice. The owl's warmth had partly melted the snow about her; this had frozen again beyond.— There's a glimpse of nature in the raw for you!

This bird is the earliest nester on this continent. By the time April arrived those infants sixty feet from the ground were eating their rabbit rations, dodging snow squalls, ignoring chillblains — *and liking it.*

The big Barred Owl, almost as large as the Great Horn, starts its housekeeping three weeks or more after the latter, yet the mother's back (and father's, since probably all the male owls help out in this distinctly feminine task, is also whitened by occasional late snowfalls. The fluffiness and depth of all owl plumage — feathered to the toes — give it a veritable cloak of eiderdown which utterly defies wind and cold. The normal blood temperature of the whole group is from four to six degrees above ours. Young owls grow to full size and become self-supporting much more slowly than do most birds; for which reason they must be hatched as early as possible — so reason the students of bird behavior, rather ignoring the fact that even in Florida and the Carolinas these two huge owls nest as proportion-

[2] It has been recently determined that — with most pairs, at least — the male Great Horn does the brooding in daytime, the female at night; the latter often being fed on the nest by her partner. But, in any event, the period over which the eggs must never become in the least chilled is 28 to 29 days; no light responsibility!

NOW THAT WE HAVE TO WALK
ately far ahead of all other birds as do their species brothers in Canada.

It is characteristic of most owl species that they become deeply attached to the comparatively small area they have once staked out as their claim, as their *lebensraum;* and they nest in and hunt through this chosen area for a decade or longer. Perhaps for life. To my certain knowledge a pair of Barreds has remained in a ten-acre piece of woods, a dense stand of hemlocks and maples, for *at least twelve years.* I have come to treat them as old friends and neighbors, near me in all weathers and seasons. Their young I have been banding with numbered aluminum bands in several successive Mays.[3] Rarely, however, do they use the same nest in consecutive years; but they do come back to old nesting sites after some years have intervened. . . . With owls in general, of all species, the annual crop of young are of course obliged to move on, starting out in late Autumn to seek their fortunes — and mates — elsewhere in the hard world. The resident adult pair, however, seem resident and seem to mate for life, till death do them part. (In this monogamous feature, owls are close to being unique among birds!) — Not like the fickle, migrating sort of birds that come and go around them.— There being no "natural" enemies of owls (—Again here the word unique almost creeps in!) home is really home to them until . . . perchance a heartless shotgun speaks — to annul the marriage!

---

[3] The author is a licensed Bird-bander, cooperating with the Federal Fish & Wildlife Service in thus serially numbering and recording trapped wild birds in the furtherance of scientific studies. This work is being curtailed by the war effort but many banders are still able to carry on restricted trapping. *Readers finding any banded dead birds are urged to report numbers to the F&WS in Washington, D. C.*

WAYFARING GEOLOGY

On Turning over a Stone

The man before me, raking the hay, had moved
A stone with the rake's prongs that curved behind.
It was a rough shale, sun-warmed on one side,
And when it tipped its cool side to the sun,
I saw the ants beneath, boiling and frenzied,
Their white and clammy eggs glistening like rice.
The red dots scurried in tormented haste.
Moments before, I thought, a regularity
Pulsed in the avenues, and over all
A sky of stone seemingly stood forever.
But a steel arm had shoved through stones and clovers,
Dodging a few and grazing others until
It found the right one. Like so many disasters
Striking in the night, this had come and passed —
And a small city shook within the weeds.
The ants' fears would be mended. For the moment,
They must know waves of fear, as others must
Who feel black scouring, whips of pain, and steel
Though not as accidental as rake-prongs.

—Daniel Smythe

CHAPTER XI

WAYFARING GEOLOGY

TAKING notice of a stone or a cliff is as provocative in its way
as taking notice of bees, or ferns, or mushrooms because
once you get into the habit you are probably in it for life.
Geology is pretty nearly as boundless as the cosmos. Most
of nature lore (like beauty, in general) is "only skin-deep"
on the body of knowledge; but launching into geology is
very much like studying anatomy. Geology is the anatomy
of the earth and you have to dig for it. By that I don't
suggest you have to go about miner-fashion with a kit of
heavy tools; no, merely that your intellect does the heavy
mining, while nearly everything you see plainly about you
as landscape has its meanings and origin farther down.

There are two quite different meanings usually scrambled
in the common use of the word; a *descriptive* geology (of a
region) is what the pedestrian sees — or could see! — while
historic geology is a vast field of knowledge and theory
built upon all the sciences, as indeed, upon all the lifetime
studies of all the world's great geologists — it is the story
of the planet and everything thereon. As basis for an
ordinary person's hobby descriptive geology of the visible
world he lives and moves about in, is *almost* enough. Yet
I am bound to state a remarkable fact, a dismaying fact,
to a naturalist: that the average human lives and moves
about in a tangible world he doesn't *really look at* at all!
Did I not firmly believe that "nothing is more remarkable
than anything else," I would call this fact the most remarkable I have ever unearthed. For years on end, the boy and
later the man may play or work in gravel pits, throw rocks,
dig ditches or excavations, scale cliffs, fish along a dozen

[*132*]

streams, climb mountains, and never have it occur to him
to stop and *look* at the anatomy of the world and try to
guess at what this and that means; to try to *understand*
what he is looking at.

In the words of Edwin T. Brewster, taken from his
absorbing book, *This Puzzling Planet:* "For so very large
an object, the earth gets curiously little attention nowadays
from the amateur of natural history. . . . Yet on the face of
things, the study of earth-science might well be the first
concern of the naturalist. . . . The geologist on a journey
has only to flatten his nose against a car window to attain
whole days of delight. . . . Altogether, for many reasons,
if one is to take up any branch of science purely for the
interest and joy of it, then our present-day geology is one
of the likely spots. . . . the only way to understand what this
earth has been like during the long stretches of the past is
to look around and see what it is like *now.*"

Along railway cuts where we have walked or ridden for
years are puzzles written among the rock strata which
should challenge the curiosity far more intriguingly than
all the crossword puzzles and information-please tests in
the papers by which the railway's passengers kill time.
The average person if he happen to be baffled by a certain
noisy bird or a certain bumptious wildflower which forces
itself on him, will be apt, in the course of time, to try
looking up its name or asking about it. Oddly not so, or
rarely so, with him who dwells half a lifetime in sight of
a hill or rock-formation which drives every visiting geologist into quick excitement. "I never happened somehow
to think about that," he will say when it is revealed to him
that he has for solving, in his very backyard, one of the
stirring detective plots of all time.

When a fellow (or his wife) starts hiking or biking
across a landscape, every hill and valley should be (but

oh so often is not) a challenge to his past schooling and future knowledge, as well as to leg-muscles and lungs. A hill is never above suspicion. No hill is just a hill; it is a resultant-of-forces. No valley is just a valley; it is a leaf from the story of things, which in its closing pages has somewhat to do with the story of the passer-by himself. Forces so vast, a story so long and intricate, that as brain-twisters, crime fictions are comic by comparison. The wayside spring also is not merely good drinking-water, but can be a thinking water too.— Start to think as you drink: "Where does this water come from; why does it appear just here?" . . . Christopher Morley it was who suggested that all travellers were of two kinds; those who travel and those who get there. Some people are all destination; some few are chiefly travellers by the way. Many years back I clipped from a pamphlet issued by our National Parks Service these brave words for the public ear: "Geology is as necessary for the comprehension and appreciation of scenery as a general knowledge of anatomy is to the painter of the human figure in action, and to the critic of his painting. Therefore, take with you to your national parks some knowledge of the great forces which nature uses in world-making and how she applies them to the shaping of the several great classes into which scenery is divided, and your enjoyment will be increased many fold. Consider this knowledge as necessary a part of your equipment, to be as carefully acquired *in advance* as your shoes and khaki and contour maps." . . .

I think I have learned one thing which is an invaluable aid to grasping the widest, profoundest generalizations in the Great Story. It is that one must try to catch a glimpse of the infinite *length* of Time, its almost infinite *slowness* — as compared with ordinary human activities. Acquiring that *one* concept is to own a tool, a talisman of understanding,

which is susceptible of a hundred applications. I might go
further to assert that probably one cannot get anywhere at
all in grasping the awesome tale, until one has divested
himself of all notions of earth-time in terms of human
history-time. There is no comparison worth drawing between the two. And, if you achieve that "time sense," to
you will be added a breadth and daring in speculation and
an incentive to theorizing which otherwise is impossible.—
For instance, suppose you stand (where in fact I did four
hours ago) looking off across a broad fertile valley (twenty
miles wide) which lies between two parallel long, single-
fold mountains — not high mountains, only some eight
hundred feet above the valley bottom — each capped by
a stratum of conglomerate rock so hard that it stoutly
resisted even the erosion of the grinding, mile-high ice-
cap of "recent" times; stand, gaze and try to realize the
truth: that once upon a time the spot where you stand was
some thousand feet *higher,* and that all the intervening
valley and the ridge opposite were *of one level then.*—
Meaning that the valley was once solid rock and soil which
has now *all* been washed out to sea, via the distant prehistoric Hudson.— That the mid-Hudson's channel was then
nearly one thcusand feet deeper, and is now filled to its
present bottom by "recent" glacial deposits.— And that its
highlands alongside were a half a mile higher than now,
having been eroded and eroded and eroded.— That the
vale of farms below today once lay in the bottom ledges
of an unthinkably massive plateau for an unthinkable time.

"Think, in this battered Caravanserai
Whose portals are alternate night and day,
How Sultan after Sultan with his pomp
Abode his destined hour and went away."

[*135*]

NOW THAT WE HAVE TO WALK

Useless knowledge, useless speculation? Yes, of course. The amateur geologist's learning is about as useless as astronomy. Yet, oddly enough, a great many men through a long time have yearned to know about suns and planets though nothing could be done with the facts. To pile useless knowledge upon necessary knowledge is the distinguishing characteristic of man's mind over that of the other primates and all other creatures. If geology is useless, in the same sense art is and so is music.

✷ ✷ ✷

At this point in my writing I took a walk up through a thousand acres of deserted hillside farmland, to the top of the tallest hill included in my rambler's lease. The hill is thirty miles long but nowhere over two miles wide. And, as I mentioned, its long summit is yet protectively crowned by that Silurian pudding-stone so gritty as to have defied the Great Ice. In the center of a scrubby pasture on its flank, I picked up a three-pound stone, the like of which in this region I never happened on before.— A stone or fragment of a stone deposited just there by melting ice, perhaps ten to a hundred thousand years ago. There it had lain all through American history and America's golden age of farming; mine probably was the first mammalian eye to be fixed on it specifically. . . . With a slide and a plunge I was shot down the geological scale to the time when no mammals had been invented, and the mammalian eye if it existed had been prematurely bestowed upon a deep-sea mollusc.

Mainly this fragment was flinty, crystalline iron ore; iron carbonate or iron sulphate, I cannot yet be sure which; and which does not matter here. About half of it had once been converted into "bog iron" (limonite). A number of exciting revelations immediately began pouring from that stone. First, that it was miles and miles from any likely place of origin; carried by the ice-raft to this lofty perch (1200′ altitude) and apparently with no brother fragments. In it the bog iron; a dark brown, fine, sandy substance whose surface bears a porous appearance; composes a vertical half of the stone; vertical, I say, because that section of the stone had two thin leaves of flint across it; true strata, though ever so thin, which had of course been laid down under water. And these leaves were at right angles to that section of the stone which had not yet been converted from the hard crystalline iron carbonate. Converted, how? By an oxidation process — probably of bacterial origin; "iron-forming bacteria" once alive and inhabiting the warm, shallow swamp water of Paleozoic times, had by their life-processes worked this miracle of chemistry. But before the whole large cliff or boulder alongside (or whatever the iron-stone mass was) could be all changed, the old swamp ceased to be — or the bacteria died, or . . .? And now, *I* was looking at it through a magnifying glass manufactured in 1941. Another striking fact was then revealed. The two thin leaves, one inch apart, of the silicious deposit of which I spoke had a third companion-leaf. But this one lay at an angle of about 15° from the other two older ones.— Then, that ancient swamp bottom had been tilted, had it not? (But not emptied.) And that tilting was a mighty slow movement. Likely a matter of centuries. There afterward underwater life again went on as usual — until its final disappearance in that swamp.

❈   ❈   ❈

Glacial Age causes have effected all the most apparent features of landscape which appear in the northern edge of the United States. That recent Ice Age sent its vast frozen sea, a mile and more thick, flowing from Labrador down as far south as Long Island on the coast (the Island is practically *all* glacial); and on through northern New Jersey, northern Pennsylvania; southwest to include all of Illinois; then northwest into North Dakota. On this line the ragged and tortuous terminal moraine lies and can be traced. Therefore, in all that ice-invaded region the greater part of the topography still bears a surface covering of the boulder-and-gravel detritus ("till") left by the melting ice — and only here and there has it been washed away since, revealing the various native bed-rocks beneath.

This circumstance provides one disadvantage and one advantage to the cursory amateur geologist of the Eastern States; it gives him a prodigious variety of different rock material to identify and also a whole landscape superimposed by the Ice Age to figure out in terms of moraines, eskers, drumlins, kames, varves, and what not — a fascinating new vocabulary. On the other hand, in these once ice-covered regions much of the native rock beneath is hidden, buried under glacial till. And it can be relatively seldom seen and studied except in such spots as cuts, cliffs, mountainsides and along large streams. Any rock one picks up among till beds or in plowed fields *could be* almost anything; it being probably a fragment of beds or lava extrusions hundreds of miles away. One's recourse here must of course be to handbooks for identification of minerals, and usually also not a little ancillary study among related sciences, even to get familiar with a starting vocabulary. Yet, as is by now well recognized, there is no royal way of lazy indifference by which *anyone* can get *anything* very satisfying achieved in the realm of Science. Even though one quickly grasps the fundamental that all rocks are *either* erupted molten stuff *or* are made by various kinds of materials laid down under water in flat beds, he as quickly finds

that such a distinction is not much of a start towards the
finer classifications. However, I believe that no branch of
science has had the benefit of so many competent and
literarily delightful "popularizers" as has this of earth-
science. In the past six years I have read at least ten books
in the general field with profit — *and great pleasure*. Not
to mention greatly enhanced insight.

❊   ❊   ❊

That concept of "a glacial age," by the way, one which is
nowadays so commonplace a truism all over the intelligent
earth, was advanced at the remarkably late date of 1840
by the famous Louis Agassiz, "father of the Glacial Theory."
Long before then geological knowledge of strata and fossils
was quite highly developed, but the investigators were
always getting stranded on what was then named "The
Drift." Presently Agassiz published a book — and it all
became foolishly simple.— Simple, I mean, in a way; *i. e.*
as to the *mechanics* of the thing, at least; if not as to the
original causes of the ice-sheet itself.— To illustrate:
There has recently come into my hands a yellowing
pamphlet printed in February of 1861 by the New York
State Museum at Albany. I feel sure that reproducing part
of a page here, eighty years later, performs some sort of
historic service. The excerpts quoted are by way of summary to the *Guide to the Geology of New York*, the text
of which exhibits remarkably developed knowledge of
marine fossils and their classification, and also of most of
the bedrocks. It seems in some particulars to reflect the
best science extant upon the age and order of the world's
strata and epochs. Yet a blind spot, real or assumed, blanks
a few of the otherwise bright pages of the little booklet.
"Science," such as it was, about that period already had

NOW THAT WE HAVE TO WALK

suffered a sharp shock from Darwin and his revolutionary evolutionary theories; and perhaps the Empire State's geologist was loath to get too far out on a limb about revolutionary theories in the geological sphere.— Yet, perhaps he had only recently heard of the "Glacial Theory" advanced first by Agassiz in 1840 (and in full in 1847) which was accepted immediately by England's geologists. Twenty-one years later he was careful to write as follows. (Following italics are all mine.)

"The natural monuments of geology *since* the Tertiary are few; the most remarkable being the enormous accumulations of gravel, sand and clay which are found so widely spread, and which are known as the Drift. This is well seen in almost *all parts* of this State, in almost *every* gravel-bank: it consists of waterworn fragments of the old rocky strata, pebbles of limestone, sandstone and slate, with some of gneiss and granite, which universally appear to have been *transported from north to south* . . . From a bushel of pebbles taken from any gravel-bank south of the Erie Canal, the geologist can pick out specimens of almost every stratum exposed north of that line.

. . . They have evidently been *transported* from north to south in *vast quantities.* They are smoothworn, and are *smaller the farther they are found from their original strata* . . . as if left by rapid currents of water. One of the most puzzling facts connected with them is, that they have been in many cases transported *from lower to higher levels,* even up steep declivities. . . There are spread with them also many large and heavy masses of loose rock called (*sic*) boulders . . . some must have come from beyond Lake Ontario.

And the surfaces of the rocky strata in all the country over which these "drift beds" have passed, are in many places found to be *worn smooth,* and *scratched and furrowed.* . . as if such heavy materials had been *dragged*

[*140*]

or driven over them. . . . Some geologists refer these facts to the operation of glaciers moving south over the country during some *supposed* epoch of arctic cold; others think the scratches were made by stones pushed over the bottom by *grounding icebergs* floating from the north while the country was submerged. Others believe they were *transported,* and the rocks smoothed and worn by violent *currents* thrown over the land from the north by some *convulsion* such as the uplifting of a great tract of northern sea-bottom. . . . It must be admitted that *none of these theories fully meets the difficulties of the case* . . .forming one of the most obscure and perplexing questions in all geological investigation."

Here we see a professional scientist of his time who demonstrates (to us) that he had most of the evidence in the case, yet could not or did not dare follow it to logical conclusions — for he *must* have heard about some of those profound conclusions reached by Agassiz. . . .

Lives there today an American who dares not speculate — even without any facts! It is an American failing; and an American strength, as well. Eager, alert, unwarped minds try to look at an old problem from a new angle. There is something childlike about this — and the adjective is not derogatory.— You remember that Tolstoi used to urge his fellow men to look at the world, to look at art "with the wide-open eyes of a child."—Perhaps it is no mere chance that Agassiz became a citizen of this country in middle age, his great European reputation behind him and preferred to finish his life here where his indomitably observant, experimental mind gave American education and science so valuable a contribution. It is generally agreed that of all our great teacher-scientists, Agassiz tried hardest always to *look at* every specimen, every "simple" problem in nature, look with the wide-open eyes of a child. Yet too often our

NOW THAT WE HAVE TO WALK

American-frontier ingenuity and clear-eyedness remain confined to factory and office; we have not learned to be a nation of amateur lookers-at-Nature, facers of life-in-general — that great field is apparently to be a vast delight saved for our future, when we "grow up" and are allowed to go out into all outdoors alone and without supervision or suspicion. So, with what surprise, freshness and sense of novelty and pioneering will Everyman some day *find* outdoor America; *see* America, with wide-open eyes *of an adult!* Out there, on hilltop and bottom-land, there may be hidden new kinds of Glacial Theories to be formulated, which as yet man does not *see,* any more than did New York's geologist eighty years ago.

SNAKE FACTS

Conversation with a Laurel

"They took me from the April woods
Among the moss and ferns;
Upon me every bud was big
With purposes and yearns.
A little soil they brought with me
Or all my sap had dried;
Some branches left, a few bruised roots,
Or else I should have died.
—Around me here exotic shrubs;
The sky is burning blue;
This humus tastes an alien tang;
The rain is rougher too."

❋   ❋   ❋

"I know. I was transplanted once
And set here where I stay,
My youthful earth was shaken loose,
My past half pruned away. . . .
In Spring we may put leafage out
And blossom — as we're bid,
But on no twig or petal show
What in our hearts is hid!"

SNAKE FACTS

A FEW years ago a well-known zoological curator delivered himself of these opening remarks before beginning a talk: "More untrue stories are told and believed about snakes than about any other group of animals. . . . Practically all snake stories one hears from the layman have no basis in fact." This statement agrees fully with my own experience and listening powers.

Undoubtedly it is true that a great many people have been kept from straying around outdoors (as once they may have longed to do) because of that common bugaboo, the fear of snakes. I meet this fear in all sorts of humans, even in strong he-men — and not city men only — as well as in womankind. The feeling is very "real"— they can *feel* the fear. It is very unnerving.— Fear of hell used to be as widespread and as fearsome.

Let us look squarely at this snake problem. In two ways fear of snake bite is analogous to fear of lightning: both are developed in childhood by adults' words and example; both these fears so seldom materialize into actual harm or death as to be hundreds of times less dangerous than motor cars on highways and bath-tubs in homes. Popular fancy imagines dangerous snakes to be common, an everywhere and ever-present menace, and that imagination keeps so many from ever becoming carefree in the country. In fact, where human beings are likely to go rambling, snakes are exceedingly few. Coiled death does not lurk under every second bush or tussock. In America dwell but three small groups of potentially "bad" reptiles; less than one-sixth of all our country's 120 species are venomous, and of these

species only five or six are at all numerous. One group in-
cludes the rattlers, one the moccasins, the other the coral-
snakes; the latter of very limited distribution.

Only three snakes of the northeastern regions of the
United States are "poison-snakes." Except in a few spots
in certain mountainous or rock-piled sections — say, in the
Poconos and Kittatinnys, the Copperhead and the northern
Timber Rattlesnake are so rare north of Mason-Dixon Line
that few inhabitants have ever seen one — I never have but
once. Probably few are eastward of the Hudson highlands
along the New York state line, and the Berkshire country.[1]
The third of the trio, the Water Moccasin (Cotton-mouth)
almost never occurs north of Washington — with the rare
possibility that there might be a few in some dense swamps
of southern Pennsylvania or southern Jersey.

Snake bite, so often talked about, seldom occurs in the
United States. The late Mr. Ditmars, undoubtedly our foremost authority, used to say that, generally speaking, reports
are few and far between concerning fatalities from poisonous snakes in their wild habitats. And that "the scarcity
of accidents from rattlesnakes may be accounted for by
the fact that they inhabit ground not serviceable to man . . .
a death from a rattlesnake-bite in the United States is so
rare as to be always first-page news."

Be prepared in advance to recognize the innocent Hog-
nosed Snake or Puff Adder, for he *looks* tough, acts tough,
at first. This snake is the biggest bluffer in snakedom — and
his head is that "triangular" kind you have probably been
taught to regard as the equipment of all deadly snakes.
Yet this snake cannot be induced actually to "bite" you.
It will puff itself up, hiss and coil and act ever so aggressive — until you get aggressive yourself. Then, like as not.

[1] Both these snakes are occasionally reported in the Blue Hills of Massachu-
setts; and the Timber Rattler is found around Ossippe, N. H.

NOW THAT WE HAVE TO WALK
after being handled it will actually "play 'possum"— act
dead. . . .

Whiskey for snake bite? — nothing could be more foolish,
more reckless. Scientific investigation has proved repeatedly
that whatever activity or drug stimulates the heart helps
to spread the snake venom more rapidly throughout the
system. Heart-beat in these cases needs slowing not
hastening.

Venom is of two types, however, one, more deadly if
not checked, acts chemically on the red blood-corpuscles
to disintegrate them. The other type is the kind which
narcotizes the nervous system. It is quite probable that the
narcotizing or slowing-up effect of this poisoning is another example of the curious way Nature has of opposing
the onset of certain diseases. Venom (type II) by at once
slowing down the heart and circulation in a way defeats
its own terrible ends.—That is, the bitten creature has this
rather fragile "defense" inherent in his mammalian biology.
Other instances of a like reaction occur when you start a
temperature: usually the fever is not to be called truly a
disease; it is rather the body's protective process of fighting
bacterial toxins; your white blood-corpuscles being more
active at higher temperatures.— Then again, in cases of
thyroid enlargement (goitre), this appears to be a physiological effort to produce more and more thyroid secretion
because in some way the thyroid gland's hormone is
being nullified by a fault of metabolism elsewhere in the
system.

As an attempted explanation of why snakes have developed the type of venom which stupifies rather than excites
a victim (— by far the common type) is that in the ancient
beginnings of its evolution snake poison rendered prey
inert and more easily managed — even as Mud Wasps
"etherize" the spiders they pack away in their mud egg-

cases to be food for the hatching larvae later; and as mother Glowworm stings her snail victims into an instantaneous paralysis before they can retreat into their shells. In the present geologic era, when venom has been evolved by snakes into an *aggressive* weapon of defense as well as a device to subdue prey, very likely their poison has not changed its character but rather has strengthened its power to the point of great deadliness. . . . Yet, if a person gets neither excited nervously — nor partly drunk — his chance of recovering from snake bite is increased by human knowledge — if not as yet wholly assured. Provided that time is on the victim's side in the early stages of the accident; a great deal hinges upon quick and efficient treatment at the very start.

Misapprehensions about snakes are many. They cannot "charm" their prey into hypnosis; nor can they so affect man, though the paralyzing fear engendered by folk-tales about them may cause a timid person "to become rooted to the spot," as the saying goes. And mankind has no "instinctive," "inherent" sixth sense which tells him of the near presence of an unseen reptile, a thing many folks believe. Snakes are not "stone deaf," but they are "as deaf as an adder,"— and are very short-sighted.[1] Venomous reptiles never "commit suicide" when cornered or fatally hurt, for — almost invariably — they are immune to their own poison and the poison of other snakes. There exists no "hoop snake" which seizes its tail in its mouth and rolls rapidly away. Contrary to usual belief, snakes do not "live till sundown" on the day they receive mortal wounds, but are comparatively easy to kill, even though that odd, automatic "electrical," muscular reflex common to lower orders

---

[1] Snakes have no outer ear or eardrum and hence are deaf to sounds transmitted through the air; they do "hear" vibrations carried through the ground.

of life, does result in a twitching and bending of a snake's body even after a mutilation as serious as decapitation.

Rattlers do not rattle with considerate intention to "warn" passers-by against possible death. On the contrary, the sound is probably a developed defensive mechanism of their own to ward off large mammals which might inadvertently kill them first.— Though it is curious as to how fear of snakes in practically all animals — which is the fact — developed through the ages, because, on the one hand individuals who died from the poison could leave no descendants and, on the other, those species or individuals who are but mildly affected by it would not be expected to have developed so marked a fear as they show. The Copperhead (often called the "land moccasin") and many harmless kinds of snakes vibrate their tail-tips in a way similar to a rattler's; usually without sound unless the trembling tip strikes against vegetation or dry leaves. The rattler's whirr is caused by the shaking together of small rings of tough, horny substance when alarmed or suspicious; it being a distinguishing peculiarity of a rattler that at every shed of outer covering an additional ring appears along its tail. The number of such rings (or rattles) does not coincide with the age in years of a rattlesnake; it sheds skin from two to four times annually, and it is also apt to lose several rattles from time to time. With the majority of specimens such calculation is impossible, says Science with finality. Every rattler is born with a "button" at its tail-tip, and it is now known that with appearance of its first ring a snake is able to rattle that button against the ring.

Another fact recently established is that extraction of a venomous snake's fangs does not render it harmless *permanently;* for it has several undeveloped fangs lying above the skin of its mouth, and a pair of these is ready for their function in two or three weeks after the first ones are removed.[2] The fangs of a snake are not really teeth any longer, but they have evolved into hollow hypodermic needles for the specific use of injecting venom. And "bite" is not exactly the word, therefore, for a serpent's attack; the act is rather a forward-driven puncture, or lancing which it performs with its two fangs. . . .

A further persistent idea holds that if one does not allow a snake to coil, it cannot strike.— On the contrary a snake rarely can strike from a coiled position. By S-bending the forward third or half of its body, nearly every snake, dangerous or harmless, may strike forward perhaps to a third of its length. No authenticated instance is on record that any serpent can jump or leap free of the ground in making its attack.

On the positive side of snake-lore, let us come to the latest recommendations with regard to treating a case of "bite." As I have mentioned, the time element is important; one must act quickly, but do the right thing. Today, after several years of careful experimentation in this country and in tropical regions, Science states flatly what is the proper thing to do in case you are bitten: by all means use, as soon as you can, *fresh, standardized* anti-toxin serum. It is called "antivenin," and is now prepared in sufficient quantities so that prominent hospitals in many large cities have a supply or can get it quickly. Most zoological gardens and natural history museums have it. The source of this product ('Lyovac' Antivenin) is the pharmaceutical firm Sharp & Dohme, Philadelphia. It can be procured from their branches in New York and throughout the country. Kits are accompanied by detailed directions. In its perfection the technique of its use is a matter for physicians to

---

[2] The Viper clan usually *shed* their mature fangs about every twenty days, anyway; at which time of course new ones are ready for immediate service at the spot.

perform. First-aid use can, however, be made by anyone. But suppose you are far from an antivenin tubule, what is to be done? Here we quote succinct directions for first-aid treatment as prepared by Mr. Ray Schrenkeisen, a lay authority on reptiles. It is a thoroughly approved treatment endorsed by medical experts:

> "If bitten by a snake, immediately apply a tourniquet between the heart and the bite. Cut deeply into the two punctures made by the snake's fangs. *Suck the wound for several hours,* or apply a suction pump. As soon as possible procure antivenin serum. . . . Most important of all is not to get excited. Excitement hastens distribution of venom through the system. The same applies to exercise or anything else which stimulates heart action."

In conclusion: If you are likely to be in a neighborhood where poisonous snakes exist, carry in your pocket the tiny serum-and-hypodermic packet now available at many hospitals and museums. It may save your life, for snake bite thus treated is very rarely fatal.— And need one say that thick leather shoes and puttees are, after all, the surest (and I don't mean *certain*) preventive against a session of pain and alarm? For, unless you are climbing upward on ledges or over rock-slides, most strikes are below the knee. . . . And certainly, if you are climbing upward among such rocky places, where sun strikes in on a warm Summer day, you might, you just *might* be wiser to take the precaution to *see* every overhead hand-hold before you grasp it — 100,000 to 1, there just *might* be a rattler there. Copperheads are near-the-ground dwellers, moccasins marsh haunters mostly, and rattlers in the east are lovers of rocks and sunny ledges. Enough said!

TALK ABOUT HOBBIES

Extreme busyness, whether at school or college, kirk or market, is a symptom of deficient vitality; and a faculty for idleness implies a catholic appetite and a strong sense of personal identity. — Look at one of your industrious fellows for a moment, I beseech you. He sows hurry and reaps indigestion; he puts a vast deal of activity out at interest; and he receives a large measure of nervous derangement in return. . . . We are in such haste to be doing; to be writing, to be gathering gear, to make our voice audible a moment in the derisive silence of Eternity, that we forget that one thing of which these are but parts: namely, to live.

—ROBERT LOUIS STEVENSON

TALK ABOUT HOBBIES

"HOBBY HOUSE."— It is my own house; a friend so christened it recently. It is also as apt a designation for three other homes I am, despite a reputation as a chronic iconoclast, permitted to enter. My own domicile is a kind of hobby-center — without in the least having meant to be. It becomes a show-off place only when some visitor insists on regarding it as such, and then only in a special sense. There is but a small amount of stuff picked up at auctions and an equally negligible amount inherited. Hand-work has yielded the normally expectable results: a garden, a lawn, an interior mostly made by hands not money. To me almost any muscular job appears so interesting that I cannot endure watching someone else's hired muscles at work on it; that I should hire others to do what I would rather do myself seems a little absurd. A few months ago I was suddenly struck by how many non-machine-made articles had been accumulated in the place — actually more in number than machine-made articles.[1] Naturally I do not purpose to publish a list of the furnishings or treasures of anybody's house and garden, but, since the Constitution guarantees to each citizen the right to choose, maintain — and publicize — a hobby, I will before I get through go so far as to enumerate how many labor-of-love products there are in this and the other hobby houses. I mean, of course, hand-hobbies and head-hobbies; handicrafts, collections, displays. . . .

It is an undisputed fact that after Pegasus got his wings

[1] A loom must not be thought of as a machine unless it be power-driven, for the loom is almost as old an invention as are polished-stone weapons.

and began to have to carry Perseus everywhere from Heaven to Hell, he ceased to be much good as a draft animal; his pinions were always getting entangled with reins and traces. He could with difficulty keep his feet on the ground. From then on, he and his rider must always be fighting the Fates, rescuing enchanted maidens, killing minotaurs; carrying on a sort of fantastic dream-life; in short, he became a hobby-horse—finally ridden to death. . . . A human with a consuming drive, a persistent tic to follow a certain trail of his own, is a little like Perseus. In every hobby there is something akin to wings. It is forever driving its rider on, higher and higher and deeper and deeper, too. An ordinary man's day is from sun to sun, but a hobby jockey practically never dismounts. Covertly — in the most innocent company — he is always "in the saddle," and with the least incitement spurs his nag and himself out of whatever pedestrian occupation he happens temporarily to engage in; from being a casual, run of the mill person, one of us, he suddenly becomes dignified into an enrapt, self-confident, wise specialist, appearing to know a great deal of which the rest of us are utterly ignorant; very much a man of the world — in that particular, minute world he has suddenly disclosed. His way of thinking and manner of speech become to an extent unintelligible except to fellow-riders; and in large measure he must express himself in figure and symbol. His speaking vocabulary is something between shop talk and sheer Greek. In contact with mortals whose wings are of another color, he is inclined to be uneasy or touchily hostile. Try it sometime: essay to enter into technical conversation, casually and airily, with such an one — you will, it is likely, neither be let down easy nor accepted fraternally, unless you present much more by way of credentials and references than merely a facile approach. Here even unctuous humility is not always

[153]

warranty of sufferance. . . . Differing hobbyists, citizens of
two realms, usually make strange bedfellows; neither of
them "sleeping a wink" because of the itching irritation
in their mutual contempt. A collector of city, state and
municipal bonds, for instance, looks with incredulous
astonishment upon a mortal who *likes* to accumulate auto-
graphs or postage stamps. And a fellow who is somewhat
daft about Lepidoptera truly believes collecting old American slip-ware a sheer perversion. A hobbyist, even more
than the usual run of humanity, secretly detests duty, and
rarely makes a hobby *of it;* and since attention to duty is
always best paid, he seldom has the income he covets.—
Some make a hobby of doing nothing; and even this avocation has a host of followers. . . . Perhaps what follows
illustrates concretely what I am driving at.

Within these particular houses I speak of (1) all the
wallpaper has vanished; (2) bricked-up, boarded-over or
otherwise ignored fireplaces, warming-ovens, built-in wood-
bins, if any; have all been exhumed and restored; (3)
carpets, linoleums and the paint which may have once
"blacked out" the original carpenter's intentions, have been
removed; (4) corner cupboards, dish cabinets, chests,
stairway rails, old furniture, doors, wainscoting, even window frames, have for the most part been deprived of their
paint — for the cult of plain wood and its graining has
risen from the dead; (5) no electric fixtures hang from
above or monopolize sidewall space so much better suited
to a painting or a print. . . . I shall have a few words to say,
seriatim, upon each innovation.

1. For half a lifetime I labored under the odd delusion
that house interiors and wallpaper went always together
like leaf and blossom, or that they were originated together
and architecturally were as lath-and-plaster joined in holy
wedlock. I am not able to guess as to the date when wall-

[*154*]

paper came in, but I know that in the days when grand-father was young plastered walls were either calcimined or white-washed, occasionally tinted, oftener not. Then I watched a neighbor take all his paper off — and it wasn't so at all; wallpaper almost never improved a room which was competently plastered. When I was obliged shortly afterward to strip one of my guest chambers of loosening paper, I resolved to paint those walls and ceiling; for the texture of that sturdy resolute old plaster was just the thing, too good to blindfold. From that time, it was a question only of how to get time to make over every room in the house.— Yet until two or three years ago when a "paint," using casein as vehicle and binder, was delivered to a wait-ing world by modern technology, the full joyful possibilities in the technique of painting interiors were not realized. Nor was the ultimate achieved in ease of application and in perfection of dull, blendable finish.

2. As for bricked-up fireplaces: apparently during the '90s tens of thousands of old homes, putting in new stoves and furnaces, cursed into oblivion the fireplaces and all that pertained thereto; it amounted to almost a mania. Who started that craze? We shall not learn now. Probably it was an indirect result of the same hypnotism of taste and straight thinking which tacked carpets to our floors, stuck paper to our walls, and wedding-caked all outside trim and porches it could reach, as well as cornices and gable-ends. How so much ill taste got launched is still something of a mystery; some say it was accomplished for architecture, at least, by the World's Fair at Chicago in 1892; others aver that the Philadelphia Exposition in 1876 set back culture in these States fifty years. Inasmuch as in initiating a new style or contraption the commonest technique used is to make present "old fogies" ashamed of what they have, this may have been just the trick played at the fairs.—

Ashamed of the finest thing in the house, the fireplace and
its fire! Extraordinary! — Like a girl in a pastor's family
being made to feel that her beauty was sinful.

3. If old floors are worn out finally and forever, even a
third-rate amateur carpenter can today lay over them a
hardwood floor of thin or thick wood; wood in which the
most beautiful grains were carefully inserted by none other
than Nature herself working in the forests. Maple, red-
grained birch, several oaks, these are manufactured tongue-
and-grooved, nail-punched too if demanded, and once laid,
need only be finished in clear varnish and heavily waxed.
But many and many an old floor throughout the Eastern
countryside is not worn out at all even if it appears to be
to an unpracticed eye, and miracles of restoration may be
wrought by a "sander" which will smooth and polish the
fine old wood.

4. It was, however, a little later than the '90s when paint
began to cover practically everything inside the house;
possibly here was working the idea that rooms should be
if possible all *in one color*. The notion of harmonizings of
several colors was not as yet widely grasped. Result is that
even to this day splendid pieces of old cabinetry and house
furnishings turn up at auctions or are for sale in isolated
homes, which bear up to three or four coats of heavy paint.
It needed no birth of "occupational therapy" to make a
lot of people who like old lines and old woods set to work
to clear all this rind from the grain of the materials. It has
been almost incredible what transformations have occurred
in even the simplest pieces of furniture or trim when they
blossom forth in the clothes given them by the trees. (Is
there not here a hint of hope that painted complexions —
which came in a whole generation after painted maple —
may go out in the same unlamented way?) Nowadays there
is great difficulty in obtaining boards of cherry, hickory,

black walnut, burled maple and clear white pine, of a size and quality that were put into handmade furniture and trim only some half-century ago. And that fact makes reclamation one of the easy ways by which to get some "antique" furniture.

5. One of the places where modern technology has fallen down, or rather, has never risen to — has it tried? — is in the transmission of electricity.— Not meaning the whole-sale transmission of it on country-leaping power-lines which often are somewhat inspiring; but referring to the retailing of that power.

Talk about Hobbies! — here is another of mine. Streets and highways everywhere suffer the ugliest desecration from overhead transmissions which in form or line lack any refinement and exhibit no concession to the beautiful — or even to the mechanical, in point of compactness and efficiency. The telephone, telegraph and light lines and their poles of our land are just as glaring, garish, sprawling and insolent where you see them duplicated in Japan, Honolulu, Peking, Perth, Italy, Switzerland or Portuguese East Africa. I suppose few really *look at* them, few *see* them, so cowed may consumers of power be by assumers of power; yet possibly they go unseen because, unconscious-ly, no one *likes* to look at them.— Rather strange at first thought that this apparently *functional* thing, wires-and poles, should appear so monstrous across natural scenery, over shrubbery and lawns, down country roads; but mon-strous it is. Its "function," however, is primarily only that of two wires carrying current; and it has no relation to linesmen's problems, the ease and cheapness of repair; these latter being challenges to production and mainte-nance which ought not to be forced upon the endurance of the public! — As if garbage were thrown into streets because it was a little difficult to build disposal-plants. For fifty

years we docilely tolerated this thing, and no one has
pulled a single wire to change it! Twenty years from now
we will be marveling that public taste could have endured
it.

Inside the home few ceiling light-fixtures have been
improved since — well, since the Pan-American Exposition,
let us say; though thorough adequacy has been accomplished in table-lamps and sidewall outlets. With modern
techniques for indirect lighting, no need exists for overhead light in rooms ordinarily low; the trend is to plug-ins
in the baseboards.

✿   ✿   ✿

Yet, after all, one's home must never become a sort of
wooden pet-dog, to be ribboned, tidied, plucked and
cleaned; worried over as if it were one's proudest possession. A house is only a complicated tool for better living.
Perhaps the simplest test for everything in it is the "test of
Nature"— *i. e.* does its form fit its function; are form and
function one? If it has no function other than being beautiful: then, if you find it beautiful, *it is.* — For you. Now. Perhaps *not* tomorrow. One never discovers form and function
at odds in Nature; but one finds often beauty *combined with*
form and function, the perfect trinity. Is it not in this sense
that your true hobbyist can bring all outdoors indoors;
that in some degree at least, he try to combine the beauty
of his heart and hand with the form and function of what
he lives most intimately with?

✿   ✿   ✿

Robert Louis Stevenson concluded: "To know what you
like is the beginning of wisdom." It is an incisive epigram.
Truly, one must have decided by sober, positive ponder-

[158]

ing; not through negative, passive acceptance; as to what form and treatment of life, of home, of art, of hobby,— of friendships — *he* himself most admires and enjoys; ere he attains the maturity of inward peace, and the outward forms of enthusiasm which flower from it.— However, I hasten to add that Stevenson's epigram carries an additional clause: "To know what you like is the beginning of wisdom — and of old age!"— By no means, whatever! Here we flatly accuse him of letting his fondness for slick rhetoric run away with his good sense. The beginning of wisdom, the onset of age? Not unless you take him to mean maturity, and not decrepitude. On the contrary, so far as hobbying is concerned to know and to do what you like is most specifically the renewal of Youth. For, as a sage more perspicacious than RLS, said: "Youth is wasted on the young." And that is far oftener a fact than your children think. . . .

Alas, so often must it be that upon reaching a certain maturity, one's own mental plant has developed the characteristic selectivity of all natural plants, that of taking to itself only those materials of its environment for which its unique metabolism has need.—An eclecticism similar to that of an animal species which is highly specialized to feed upon only one or a few organisms. A certain man takes a walk afield and what mainly he sees, notes, remembers is what he already knows most about, cares most about; the botanist sees plants, the bird lover, birds, the geologist, rocks and contours. To all else each is largely anesthetic. Side by side in my garden grow cucumbers and sweet corn; from the same soil-water what a different osmosis draws life to each. . . . There used to be a city-mind and a country-mind with regard to life's hobbies, pleasures and relaxations. But by this date the meridian between them has all but vanished in many rural latitudes; gasoline has dry-

[159]

cleaned it from the map. Out here the all-day radio runs on
and on; its urbanized entertainments: theatre, concerts,
night-clubbing, vaudeville sound in every farm home.
When supper is over; if anywhere, the car to town (having
choice of several towns); the roadhouse, the movie, bingo,
treasure-night, etc. — Aboard Bagdad's magic carpet woven
of filmstrips, to Shangri-la.

The 1890-1910 neighborhood home or barn dance
among the farmers, the rural 'sociable,' the evening around
the neighbor's organ — song, cider and popcorn — are, like
the Winter straw-ride, as dead as the 15th Amendment in
Mississippi. And the country, as country, seems hardly to
appeal any more to its residents. In the last fifteen years of
my own non-highway walking hereabout, almost daily and
over a wide terrain, I have seen or met (away from the
roads) *but one country dweller* taking a walk for the fun
of it! — That one was a fifty-year-old, foreign-born Italian
mother of four — who was wearing her husband's work-
shoes. These were all they owned between them fit for
rough going.

That city people, on their part, are ever increasingly and
ever more eagerly looking toward the dances, the songs
and the music of the hillbilly, the cowhand, the rural negro
and the Eastern dirt-farmer for "regional culture" and
habitant vocabularies, is true too. As I see it this merging
of the non-workaday interests of town and country is an
irreversible process. The auto, the movie, the radio caused
it; will perpetuate it. Out of it eventually must come a new
sort of hybrid culture. (Whatever will it be like!) There has
been for a decade in every large city in the East a steady
rise in the number of and membership in hiking-clubs,
trail-clubs, so-called "nature groups" subdividing into
museum groups, bird groups, botanical groups and so on.
(Not to mention Boy and Girl Scout groups. Nor to point

TALK ABOUT HOBBIES

out the marked revival in popularity of the rural reels and square-dances among urban young folks.) So there is the amusing possibility that through Cityman's enthusiasm, Countryman may be provoked into a renaissance of interest in the countryside and its out-of-doors!

Handicrafts and Hobbies represented in the Hobby-Houses

(CHECK ONE!)

Woven Rag Rugs
Wood Carvings, in relief or in the round.
Color-Prints by screen process.
Linoleum-Cut Printing (Used on Christmas cards, textiles, tablecloths, sofa cushions, curtains, et cetera.)
Woven Window Curtains
Carved Book-Ends
Brass Book-Ends, Cutout or hammered metal
Copper and Brass Dishes
Pottery Statuettes
Bookshelves, broad, built-in
Book-Binding
Woven Bedspreads

Patchwork Quilts
Hooked Rugs (and chair seats)
Clay Modelling
Wooden Chest Making
Zinc Etching
Dyeing, curtains, old shirts, ties, hats, other garments
Tie-Dyeing
Batiking
Basketry, willow, raffia, hickory
Painting in Oils
Lithography Prints
Photo-Montage
Built-in Woodwork
Box-Bedsteads (red cedar)
Postage Stamp Collecting
Flower Gardening

❃   ❃   ❃

Suggested Lines of Nature Interests

Wild-life Photography
Bird-Nest Collecting
Vivariums
Insect Galls

Mineral Specimens
Edible Wild Plants
Aquariums
Fungi

[*161*]

NOW THAT WE HAVE TO WALK

All Orchids of the Region

Woods Garden

Weather-Chart

Box-Trapping Mammals for Study

Frogs, Toads, Turtles of Region

Observation Beehive

Hokum Encyclopedia (nature nonsense)

Attracting Birds (research)

Bird-Banding (after War is over)

Bat Housing Project (don't laugh, try it; it has never been done! Original contributions to science possible.)

Ferns of the Region; Fernery

Bird Migration Table

Salamanders of the Region

Indoor Ant-Hill

Concrete Outdoor Pool

Moths of the Region

Microscopic Nature

Insect-Rearing

Puzzle-List (nature puzzles and queries)

Mole Study (here original contributions to science possible.)

Microscope Photography

"Ingenuity is never slaked; hobbies are never finished."

❋　　❋　　❋

Bird Feeding as a Hobby

The entertaining hobby of feeding birds in winter around our homes is being resorted to by an ever increasing number of us. It's a fine idea; fine for the birds, fun and interesting for the providers. If a few obvious precautions are taken the feathered feeders show little reluctance to come to meals and are in no great hurry to depart. Here are offered a number of gadgets and contraptions to fit into almost any local conditions. All of them are tried-and-true; they have all seen service under veteran bird enthusiasts.

The first one is picturesque as well as practical. Saw a cocoanut into halves. It should be a "ripe" one; a nut inside which most of the milk has hardened into a thick lining of meat. For you may hang the halves roundside up by a string from a radio aerial, telephone wire or tree branch and let the boarders pick out the cocoanut meat. After that food is exhausted (and, as we'll see in a moment, it is not a highly acceptable food) you refill the shell with something better; in both cases it is important that a short stick be inserted *slanting-wise* into the filling in order to afford a perch for the eating bird. This sort of food-holder sheds rain and snow and keeps the provender from dirt and leaves.

But for a more desirable kind of bird food make the following: Melt down a generous amount of liquid beef suet from the chunks you can get the meat man to give you. Stir into the warm liquid a mixture of chopped or mashed nut meats, minced raisins and a little ground lean meat. While the delicacy is warm enough to pour, fill the emptied cocoanut shell halves with it and allow it to cool. Just before it hardens insert the wooden skewer or branch into it at an angle — a six-inch length is sufficient. (A small screw-eye inserted in the shell serves to carry the suspending string or picture-wire.) This food mixture is a general-purpose delicacy liked by most all small birds except the seed-eaters.

For a variant of the halved cocoanut, use a whole one as follows: make a 1¼ inch round hole through the shell (and meat) on opposite sides at the "equator" of the nut, suspend it, then allow the Chickadees, Woodpeckers and Nuthatches to clean it all out for you. To refill again and again if need be, pour in the before mentioned suet mixture. If cocoanuts are hard to come by in your locality nowadays, a fair substitute is one of those heavily paraffined drinking cups of paper. These rarely last long enough to refill — and, by the way, do not put much mixture into them on account of its weight.

A fourth idea is to secure a few dry limb-crotches from the woods, choosing V-shaped pieces (about two inches in diameter) with one leg longer than the other. Bore augur holes two or three inches apart into the wood and fill these with suet mixture by means of a spatula or putty knife. The crotches can be hung over any convenient wire or branch in such a manner that they will not be blown off by the wintry winds. The less freely the sticks swing about, the better — from a bird's point of view. This stick offering is a special temptation to the Downy Woodpeckers. . . . Here's another suggestion: unrotted pine cones, the bigger the better, can be dipped into lard or that selfsame suet mixture, and when cold and dry are to be suspended here and there just like the rest of the food-holders. Chickadees are fond of this way of feeding.

I have not mentioned the feeding-shelf supported against the side of a tree or nailed on a windowsill, and provided with all manner of bones, seeds, fruit and scraps, for the reason that it is so very well known and used. But all birds patronizing such artificial restaurants will like their bill of fare as well if it is put inside woven, coarse-meshed orange or candy bags. Such can be hung from a nail on a trunk or hung from something overhead. Suet chunks and soup-bones are ideal for these grab-bags.— Then again, you could hang up whole pig or sheep hearts (as the Germans abroad used to do) — only you must not till after the war! — a fare which provides a lot of lean meat as a change from too much fatty material. Certain birds, those with powerful beaks, like Jays and Grosbeaks, enjoy the chance to get out the nuts from festoons of peanuts-in-the-shell strung upon heavy pack-thread among the branches of evergreen trees. A few shells should be cracked so that the birds readily "get the idea."

It is not too difficult to make a few bird-doughnuts to hang out.— I do not mean the kind of crullers *you* like to dunk, although even these go pretty well with the bird customers — until they break to pieces. I mean a life-preserver-shaped ring of food hung up outdoors. You go at making it this way: for a mould you take an empty *wide* coffee can, and you set in the center of it something like a section of cardboard mailing-tube — this last in order to fashion the hole of the "doughnut"— you then pour into the can bottom an inch or so of that suet mixture we have been referring to. Leave the cardboard lining in when you remove the now hardened outside suet-ring, because it will serve as reinforcement to prevent the hanging-up string from cutting its way through on warm days. This goody is usually eaten by the visitor when perching inside the hole; a very enticing little spectacle to watch,— *and* photograph!

An easy-to-make but in many ways ideal feeding table consists of a large pan secured to the top of a tall wooden two-by-four or pole by a nail through its bottom. A few holes punched also in the pan allow rain and snow water to drain out. Into this pan you put anything and everything you dream a bird might fancy (It's *never* bread or crackers!) — ex-soupbones rich with marrow, a piece of apple, a chunk of suet, seeds for the seed-eaters, etc. If set in, by aid of a crowbar, in mid-lawn or opposite your windows so that the pan's level is at least six feet up, cats cannot climb over the rim or jump to catch feeders from the ground.

And so we come to cats! Any gadget which you put up must be calculated so as to be out of reach of cats — no question about that! And of squirrels also, for they are fond of your food supply, rather than fond of the birds, as cats are, and will soon deplete the larder.— But, then, perhaps you'd like the squirrels to come anyway. Another point: *if placed in direct sun*, suet mixtures will be apt to melt.

Seed-eaters among birds rarely will eat anything else.

NOW THAT WE HAVE TO WALK

Pheasants, Tree Sparrows, juncos, Goldfinches, Snow Buntings, etc. can be entertained *in wide open spaces* (again because of cats!) by scatterings of such provender as rapeseed, sunflower seed, mixed scratch feed (prepared for poultry), corn, and packaged canary mixtures. By devising a small lean-to of boards over the feeding station the ground will be kept dry and free from snow.

Don't worry that you will make "parasites" of birds by feeding them, so that they won't be so able to take care of themselves later on; or that they will make themselves sick by over-eating. Apparently these sad consequences never do follow.

More commonly than the beginner realizes, his hobby supports one or more publications; to some of these he should subscribe. More likely than not such periodicals are published as non-profit-making activities by the members of some association or group of those engaged in the hobby, or investigation, or angle of science to which the beginner is attracted. Membership in such groups is urged by the author.

As a case in point: When several years ago I began to do bird-banding, as a licensed co-operator with the federal Fish & Wildlife Service, I had no clear idea as to the number of my fellow-workers in this project, nor whether any were located near me, nor how much and what already had been learned from the nation-wide experiment. It was not long before I discovered that not only was there a regular government publication summarizing progress, and three regional Banding Associations, but also that the geographically local group, to which I soon attached myself, prepared a mimeographed monthly "magazine" or news-letter. Moreover, that for a trifling additional sum the printed monthly of the Northeastern States Association would be sent me. The amount of information thus available, emanating as it did from several thousand students, scientists and/or hobbyists, had a very stimulating influence upon my understanding and my practices in the field.

. . . The hand that rounded Peter's dome
And groined the aisles of Christian Rome,
Wrought in a sad sincerity;
Himself from God he could not free;
He builded better than he knew:
The conscious stone to beauty grew. . .

—EMERSON

CHAPTER XIV

SEVENTEEN YEARS AND A DREAM

THE lot of a certain boy fell among trees. He lived and grew among trees. Trees which seemed to him forever. Trees summergreen and evergreen. And the shape, the size, the color and the meaning of trees somehow became his; sealed and set apart in a secret sector of his being. All this he did not know while he was yet a boy, nor that his highroad was to be lined by trees; that in the end he would come to dwell among them again — and they in him. . . .

A young man held a picture in his mind's eye so long that finally the memory became a dream in his heart, a goal for his ambition. The picture was of trees: trees along a river; on a hundred hills and mountain slopes; cathedral-like forests; forests of trees roundabout a town, planted by it and owned by it.— The *planted* forests of Europe.

That memory of tannenbaum, larch, fir, pine, particularly in Germany and Switzerland, never faded thereafter. The man found no trait to be more characteristic of old German folkways and culture than their deep love of trees; of walking, sitting, conversing among them.— Nor was delight in trees confined to the Germans; there were for Czechs, Swiss, French, Belgians, probably others, public forests and forestry as a matter of course. Perhaps this feeling for forests, a subtle influence, went back even to ancient days when as tribes before Roman civilization came they lived in the dark woods, the primeval Great Forest of Europe. Hardly now an old city, from small to great, whose environs were not ringed by planted forests, heirlooms, most of them, of generations. They were there not only for beauty and pleasure, but as assets, sources of lumber in perpetuity. . . .

NOW THAT WE HAVE TO WALK

The man found surprise in all this; to him a new way in men that they should make, own, love forests; in America woods were counted of value only when axed, sawn and sold; when the land they encumbered could be cleared of them and *used*. Yet abroad the people had transformed a city's surroundings — not alone into something like a park, wide and informal; but more, into quiet, solemn, lovely woods which invited the soul to meditation, rest, or social gathering together. . . . This, he felt sure, was good. Americans did not do this; they seemed unaware of something deep and fine in forests. And in human intercourse.

The Dream which came out of the memory, was of *trees in America*. He would, himself at last a trained forester, set out many trees, to grow into a forest, in the midst of which he might one day build a home, perhaps; a forest which would be as beautiful in itself as in its threefold purposes:

As sanctuary and refuge he would

> ". . . give, bequeath, devise
> Shelter to every bird that flies;
> Harbor to all that walk or creep;
> To the red fox a bed for sleep;
> Table and roof for every guest
> And place for dove and thrush to nest. . ."

as restitution to or salvage of soil which his forefathers had raped, then scorned. As appeal, silent and tangible, that such a forest be example and incentive to his fellow citizens to perceive a new graciousness in the art of living; that Americans might at long last repossess something which in moving to another continent they had lost or mislaid.— Presumptuous and grandiloquent program, as distant from realization as was Europe across the sea — very like the

[*170*]

one Thoreau spoke of: "The youth gets together his materials to build a bridge to the moon, or perchance a palace or temple on the earth, and at length the middle-aged man concludes to build a woodshed with them."— America did not care a shingle what anyone thought of her, she with beauty laid on all over her lusty features; tilting the chin of Omnipotence and smirking down into its eyes.— As for wild life; it was "doing all right." . . .

In later years it came to pass that an obscure ancestor willed him an equally obscure farm; fragment of a farm, rather; which, from an original 180 acres in the days of the Civil War (when men who had not gone South were going West), had been hacked down to thirty. He looked upon it and found that it was — not so bad. Scanned its four separated areas of cleared but fallow land, fourteen acres in all; and knew from the outset that on the one hand, tillage was futile, or heartbreaking; on the other, that, lacking it, two or three years would see field-birch, briers, wild grape and thicket upsurging triumphant. Fourteen acres — why, marginal land *to plant trees on* — *what else!* . . . The Dream was taking shape. . . . That was seventeen years ago.

*   *   *

Six years passed. The Spring was of the seventh year. The work of the world had been going on. Life had been busy and preoccupied. The man had been abroad again, this time to the ends of the world, and he had returned to the place in the evening before. When he arose from bed and looked out the Great Revelation broke. Came the apocalypse of his Dream! — It was almost as if one awakened on a Spring morn (as in the fairy stories) and happening to look casually, calmly from the window of his chamber, he suddenly beheld *an enchanted forest!* — Some-

thing a jinni had conjured forth in a night! Young trees,
shapes of beauty, where you remembered clearly should be
meadow grass, with dashes of sumachs and siftings of
blackberry.

Now out there hiding the hillsides, rank on rank, garbed
in virgin greens touched by the light of a gilded dawn,
reaching out into new burgeoning, new life, growth, youthful pine trees and spruces, eternal symbols of Easter; of
the ancient, most primitive Eostre: the figure and form of
fertility. As if supplicating Eostre the resurrection deity,
goddess of the vernal equinox; their rising sap, their rising
spires saluting the rising sun in a concert of aspiration and
hope. . . . The man who had set them there stared and
stared — until the vision dissolved in very unmanly tears.
Truly it was an overpowering realization on that sun-shot
morning that he once, long ago, had said in his heart: let
there be a young forest here! — *and a young forest was
there!* Throughout the years that had passed among men,
out there the conscious field to beauty grew; he had planted
better than he knew. Nature had responded ten times tenfold; he had given a four inch twig with roots, had asked
of her a few saplings — and lo, she had returned to him a
forest! . . .

From time to time in this Seventeenth Year there come
visitors to this place of green wonder; men and women not
a few, from divers stations and walks; and each is unpre-
pared and unknowing what manner of temple Nature is
erecting here. The poet, the forester, the conservationist,
the farmer, the warrior, the artist, the naturalist — and the
cubicle-and-desk refugee; here all these, like pilgrims, may
enter thick-carpeted aisles along leaping columns set overhead into groined arches of limbs. As though from high
windows fall broad shafts of sunshine. The gray-green-
brown interior, vast and mysterious, is dim-lighted into a

SEVENTEEN YEARS AND A DREAM
variegated symphony of a dozen shades and tones; and
escutcheons of gold hang upon all the walls and pave the
floor. As far as he can see, the rolling needle-spread earth
is now a kneeling place for worshippers. From aloft the
soft passing of the breeze; from every side the calls of
birds. . . . The pilgrim has not very far to go now before
he realizes he is in a holy place. He stands to wonder, to
look, to listen — and then into his heart falls some little
fragment of that dream which once was only another's.

❋   ❋   ❋

You Can Do It Too.

The author outlines below the main steps involved in
starting a reforestation project; a procedure which virtually
duplicates that followed by him seventeen years ago. It is
suggested as a part time or spare time project for a family
who can or will own some acreage or a home in the country,
no matter how pretentious or unpretentious it is. Such a
project is in line with conservation, a public service of real
importance; it yields dividends of many kinds, including
beauty, permanence and the enhancement of the real estate
values. . . .

Into the author's tracts some 15,000 seedlings had gone;
scotch pine, red pine and, interspersed, that most perfect
Christmas tree, norway spruce. And now, eighteen years
after planting, here stood a forest, its units forest trees; it
was the Forest I wanted from the beginning. All paid for,
and a clear asset for a century to come. Almost stranger
than all else, most paradoxical of all, despite philosophy
and physics, a man had been able to eat his cake and have
it too.— How was that?

[*173*]

NOW THAT WE HAVE TO WALK

While the saplings were small, the best but four feet high, the rest harboring no presumption to rise above my head; the stand yet only suggesting a forest; one Christmas season a horde of buyers demanding Christmas trees descended upon my astonished acres like locusts out of the prairies; and I had been able to supply some of them by thinning out a tree here, a tree there. During the years following it was possible — indeed, I learned, sound forestry practice required it — to stagger out alternately and sell as Christmas trees of all sizes, nearly 600 of the spruces. Thus, in all, over $700 was received; the cost of the entire project; taxes, upkeep, planting; repaid twice over. Yet in the end, when all cutting ceased — no sign remained of that thinning process! Growth of trees had widened to cover all the spaces. . . . Here faultlessly stood the woods — originally the hope and intent of the dream. It was obvious that in the very beginning I should have guessed the possibility of this lucrative bonanza, but I did not.— Remarkable how inconspicuous the "obvious" sometimes is!

Planting a small forest of evergreens is gone about as follows: the huge tree-nursery (probably) maintained by your State Conservation Department furnishes you "seedlings" (two years old) and/or "transplants" (three or four years) of several appropriate varieties, selling them "at cost," say from three to five dollars per thousand respectively; both are very small. Transplants are to be preferred.— By law, you are prohibited from ever selling these trees with roots upon them, since, of course, they are intended for foresting and not for ornamental uses.

These are shipped at the proper season, full planting directions either accompanying or having been contained in State or Federal pamphlets on the subject. When your order was sent in and accepted months before, Spring planting having been decided on, you asked undoubtedly

[174]

for one or more of the following species, in multiples of a
thousand plants:

Scotch Pine	Native Spruce (white, black or red)
White Pine	European Larch (tamarack)
Red Pine	Norway Spruce White Cedar

Through information contained in such pamphlets — or
you obtained it through correspondence — you were guided
as to what species you ordered. A determining factor is
the general character and quality of the soil to be used.
The planting process is just about the same for all.

1000 to 1200 trees may be planted per acre, if set
six feet each way from one another, in straight rows.[1]
Making holes and setting in the little trees is not over-
arduous work, nor does it necessarily demand previous
experience or an exacting technique.— Though, make no
mistake, knack and knowledge always fatten upon experience. In particular, what makes the whole task more
difficult and lengthens it, is a terrain used which is overgrown very much with vines, brush, briers or heavy-weed
growth. Setting in baby trees in meadow, poor or good, or
in well-grazed pasture is easiest. There is very little sense
in attempting afforestation in land heavily shrubbed and
well on its way into thicket.— Or attacking swale, marshy
lowlands or swamp, except after expert guidance. For in
these latter situations the freeze-and-thaw of Winter and
early Spring invariably heave out a high proportion of your
roots. Even a little dampness in a given spot acts in that
way.

Your soil need not be fertile; in fact, evergreens do better
in the long run on "worked out" or marginal areas — and
by that I do not mean gravel-pits or sand dunes! Planting

[1] See end of chapter.

NOW THAT WE HAVE TO WALK
in April instead of early September is preferred because in
Spring soil is usually well supplied with moisture, rain is
frequent. Never try to do it in Autumn unless specifically
advised to do so by an expert — be sure it's *an expert*. That
your rows be straight is important; you will have *staked
them out* in advance.

Planting is a two-man job; one makes the setting holes
(they are horizontal rather than *deep* holes, oddly enough),
the other sets and firms. A second setter can often be used
if the man who wields the heavy mattock is able to keep
ahead of two. Four swinging cuts lay open a gash through
and below the turf, every six feet, three or four inches deep;
the setter lays his root in loose earth, packs the dirt deftly
around and above; laying on top if possible a loose cover
of broken turf, to prevent sun-drying. A shoe pressed heavily
down on two sides to prevent rain-washing; and your
seedling is planted.

If the setting out was properly done, and normal average
rainfall followed during this and the second Spring and
Summer, the mortality rate on level areas should run no
higher than five per cent the first year; with perhaps three
per cent more in a second year. During the second and third
Springs replacements are to be made, filling the gaps.
Attempts to fill in after the third Spring are usually a waste
of time because the older trees in a few more seasons so
shade the younger sisters that they turn out weak and reedy.
With each year the rate of growth accelerates somewhat;
by the tenth the ground will receive little sunshine, so that
grass and weeds are being blotted out; by the twelfth a
start at trimming off lower limbs (if desirable) becomes
possible. This decreases fire-hazard. Meanwhile, through
the first decade, brush and briers if they exist must be
kept down with clippers every other year. A task which
requires less man-hours than would be supposed — perhaps

[*176*]

not more than two dollars worth per acre annually. After
Year Ten virtually all alien growth is prevented by the
shade of the trees themselves. . . . After twenty years the
stand should carry on permanently, if trunks are finally
staggered to twelve feet each way; unless soil conditions
are favorable enough to nourish a closer stand.

There are RISKS. First among them is fire. Secondly
come cattle trespass; and if they are about, the grazing and
barking of the small trees by deer. A third risk is that of
large-scale theft if tract is accessible to roads and not overseen all through the year, especially towards Christmas.
Insects and disease are, of course, possible, but their occurrence is rare, except in certain areas. The major damage
in most places comes from the weevil borer whose eggs
are laid in the apical bud just as growth stops, its larvae
soon emerging and burrowing[2] down, down, right to the
very end of the last old growth; immediately followed by
the death of the new growth. A mutilation which causes
zigzagging of the trunk. In most of its old, original habitat
our magnificent White Pine cannot be afforested at all
because of this damage. . . . If a reader is debating whether
or not to try a bit of forestry on his own, he had best secure
more technical and detailed information from his State
authorities than I can set down here. I may however add
that experience is more pedagogical than theory and advice.

✿   ✿   ✿

The above outlined procedures are the generalized,
standard practice, especially for a plantation of not over
ten acres. I must suggest, however, a variant scheme — the
"Christmas tree scheme"— which I can state from personal
experience, has been very successful:

If (1) the tract is within fifteen miles of a city, and not

2 This borer attacks only Spruces and White Pines.

far off a road, and (2) *if* it can be closely overseen and protected from fire and especially from theft.

The plan suggested is the one which the author would follow himself were he in possession of any more land to plant evergreens on; and were he still avid "to have his cake and eat it too." (In other words, the present scheme is a commercial one mainly.) The plan is one designed for a small plantation; if one's acreage is much greater than six acres, he begins to operate (commercially, that is) on a *wholesale* basis; whereon all matters of selling, cutting, and costs generally, as well as profits, are beyond the pale of this proposition.

I would plant each acre in double rows made up of multiples like this:

```
     (4ft.)    (4ft.)    (4ft.)
       o     x     o     x
                              ) 6
                              ( ft.
       x     o     x     o
```

o – Red Pine
x – Norway Spruce (the world's perfect Christmas tree)

The reasons are these: If you want to cover all the costs of your project, including cost of the land, you can sell Christmas trees every season for about eight years in all; and you can sell them to city people who will delightedly come out in their automobiles to select them personally, will pay you a high retail price, and will return year after year. So you will want to get into your future forest as many Spruces as you can scientifically take out; and if that wording sounds odd, read on.

1. Since many of your spruces will reach table-size early, 7 to 8 years, and since there is heavy demand for this size,

you can thus (p. 178) grow many of them. You get an income early.

2. Yet, as larger sized spruces, 6 to 9 feet, bring twice as much each, you want a maximum of yours to grow a *longer time*, hence the *removing* of many of the small ones has left the others space enough to develop uncrowdedly and hence perfectly.

3. In the end (meaning after about 18 years) after you have sold some ¾ of all the spruces — and ¼ of them will not develop a shape good enough to sell — you have left mostly Red Pines, your best long-term timber asset. But you have left also enough spruces scattered through to add greater beauty and variety to your forest.

If you think your market will be a large enough one to enable you to dispose of a great many Christmas trees (and remember that as the years go on now, good trees will get scarcer and scarcer) you might wish to plant your trees this way:

```
      o     x     x     o     x     x     o
 6 ⎧
ft. ⎩
      x (4 ft) x (4 ft) o (4 ft) x (4 ft) x (4 ft) o (4 ft) x
```

In either event, you probably can't lose; certainly the country won't lose; and (if you had heard what I have from hundreds of buyers) the customers haven't lost by securing the finest and freshest-cut specimens of Christmas tree to be had. Good luck!

Soaring Hawk

Sail ho! — What ship? . . . But on she steers
Across the Turquoise Straits
Through the Archipelago of Clouds,
Deep with gossamer freights.

From winds I cannot feel below
Her straining sails are taut;
She lays a course beyond my shores —
Aye, past my farthest thought!

What compass points you? — If you trade,
What cargo homeward bring?
Spoke you my Ships, my golden Ships?
—And were they prospering?

CHAPTER XV

ANIMAL INFANTS

That Defender-in-Chief of canines, the fay and funny
James Thurber, trenchant and defiant towards dogmas,
wrote in praise of dog-mothers in general: "They prove how
much happier the parent-child relationship can become if
managed without fuss, sentiment or worry. . . At six
weeks the mother dismisses the children from her mind
and is free to devote herself to her career."

ONE would not need to single out pups as recipients of sane
motherhood. The possession of what could be honestly
named true — and sane — mother love, I believe to be the
rule and not the exception among mammals and birds.
It is not infrequently accompanied by paternal solicitude
of a high order. The tenderness and brave attention rarely
if ever approaches coddling or over-indulgence; or, above
all, that way of treating one's helpless offspring as if they
were cunning pets, born largely for parental delight and
amusement — an attitude too common in my circle of
acquaintances.

Such wilderness care and solicitude are never aimless,
never sentimental. Though at times obviously tender (no
other word for it!), these parental attentions strike me as
in general more efficient (and purposeful, maybe) than
our own. The intense, intricate emotional involvements of
some human mothers with their children find no parallel
in routines of outdoor nurseries.— Of necessity it must be
so in a state of nature. During the infancy of nature's young
much which passes as "training" has to be compressed into
a few weeks, whereas we human parents perforce must

worry and wonder on for years, with no instincts to help us and no standardized model of finished product to work toward. So brief is wild parenthood, so instinctive its guidance, that little leeway exists for corrections of parental "mistakes," if made. Little time to attempt thwarting those inherent instincts with fussy alarm and impulsive guesswork, as we not rarely do.

Call it instinct — though naming is not explaining — that the adult birds provide the correct type of food for each growing-stage of the nestling, with no errors seemingly ever made; call it only instinct which at exactly the proper time brings about lessons in exercise, flying, fleeing, hiding, stalking; it surely is a fact that side by side with mother love a competent, daring protection and assistance do operate. The fact is even more evident among mammals.

Once I was lucky enough to get a moving glimpse into a bit of mothering by a woodchuck, one of those lowly, common, timorous rodents about which every country person imagines he knows everything and which he thinks is a dumb, dull, shootable pest. Motoring briskly along a fairly well-travelled highway, I suddenly saw a little group of furry brown animals crouching in the grass by the roadside. Only a second's glimpse it was, but I felt there was something worth stopping to investigate. I left the car a few rods further, and while walking back saw a charming sight: led by mother chuck carrying one six-inch baby by the nape like a kitten, three other toddling youngsters slowly single-filed straight across the road. By the time I reached the place mother began scrambling up the steep bank which there flanked the highway, to disappear above with her precious burden. The three, either warned to wait or dismayed by the impossibility of scaling the bank, were huddled at its bottom scared, wide-eyed and motionless. I stood right over them but they moved not at all, only looked up at me

[182]

ANIMAL INFANTS

from large beautiful brown eyes, and waited in utter
helplessness what this great giant would do to them.

I never saw such winsome creatures! No larger than
three-week-old bunnies and of practically the same color,
their infant appeal was irresistible. A flow of feeling came
over me which instantly changed a tense, hurrying motor-
driving man, centered in his own so-important pursuits in
a competitive world, into a — well, into a sort of maternal
human organism.— That queer state which probably most
of us have sometimes experienced, has never been described
better than by Ivan Sanderson in his *Animal Treasure:*
"The inner lining of my body seemed to grip me as if
prepared to rack me with tears, with pain, with gay laughter
all at once. You alone know how you feel when you see
some little fragile thing, so sweet and gentle and pathetic
that you want to seize it to you, caress it and squeeze it
into your very self — it is the secret of Walt Disney's car-
toons, the basis of mother love, the very essence of sympathy and compassion."

Emotional confusion checked me for a few moments
irresolute; then driven by this deep impulse I bent over
slowly and stroked one quivering brown back (it quivered
only after my touch) half-fearing a nip or a wild stampede.
Neither happened. Presently I closed my fingers around a
tiny chuck, lifted him and held him encircled in my hand.
I fondled him softly with the other, could feel the flutter
of his little heart, sense his great fear. But he did not struggle
nor did the others on the ground stir where they crouched.
Mother was gone. Perhaps she had left some stern injunc-
tion that they stay just there, where they could be found
later. Her decision was the one practical thing to do; to
escape with at least one infant, and later if fate allowed,
to return for these who also had to be carried up the steep
slope.

[183]

NOW THAT WE HAVE TO WALK

To leave them there by the traveled highway was certain danger. I climbed with them one by one and settled them deep in the tangled grass above. . . . I hope that mother chuck did reunite them in some safe hole which most probably she had gone ahead hours to locate. Possibly the soaking downpour of the past night had flooded the original burrow and obliged her to move the young at daybreak. — Competent motherhood; perfect infant behavior!

A few weeks later, far from this adventure, while ranging hill-pastures near home I happened to point my binoculars at a distant chuck perched on its burrow mound. There flashed into view a bit of tender beauty as moving as the other. In the golden light of sundown a brown mother sat upright on her haunches, a forward leg and paw embracing a half-grown infant which stood nursing at her breast. A perennial symbol of motherhood. Almost, it seemed, she too — as a woman might — was daydreaming of what the years might bring this wee bairn of hers. . . .

Surely the greatest delight in observing animals comes from watching young ones of wild families together unaware, unafraid. *Snow White* swept the country like a blizzard due to its "human interest"; that is, animal-interest, the whimsical, childlike pranks of animals-as-people. After one has watched a mother skunk leading a file of four black and white kittens, nose to tail, through dewy meadows at twilight, one gains new sympathy for skunks (how they need it!); prejudices give way to better impulses as you see her industriously grubbing out insect food for them as a hen works for its chicks, now and again making tiny calling sounds (very rarely at other times do skunks make any sound), ever alert and instantly on the defensive if an enemy appear. And, under such conditions, she never makes that dignified slow retreat characteristic of lone

[*184*]

ANIMAL INFANTS

skunks, but boldly steps in front of her young and offers attack.

Last summer I was camping out beside my car far from home, in a V-shaped bit of overgrown pasture lying between the confluence of two trunk highways, not ten miles from a large city. At sunset I was sitting on a rocky outcrop in the center of what *had been* pasture, say ten or twenty years back. Now all about me were starved grass, scanty bayberry, hardhack, scanty gray birches, thornapple clumps. The passing of traffic made a low sullen roar twenty rods away. A most unprepossessing spot this, but owing to the exigencies of the trip it had to do for a one-night-stand. . . . Suddenly I caught a faint movement thirty yards distant. Not until some seconds passed was I aware that it was an animal. A buffy-brown-and-black creature faced me. All at once, like a negative crystallizing out of the developing-bath, it emerged from its background — what I had first taken to be a foraging cat became a gray fox. (This species is *not* gray — but that is the name it bears!) . . . It stayed still. A moment or two passed — and a second fox walked up, playfully touched noses with the first and began coaxing it to romp. I was not seen. The lithe things played there, more like kittens than pups, long tails rippling, curving about. Leaps, somersaults, crouches, intervals of waiting for an opening. . . .

So attentive was I to the pair that I failed to notice the arrival of a third actor, until a rolypoly fuzzy cub tried to join in the scrambling. This was impertinence: one of the elders, leaping high over the other, scooped the baby with one flashing paw and sent it rolling into the bordering high grass.— *Well*, at that instant the grass seemed alive with fox cubs, for no less than four began a free-for-all tussle among themselves, and soon popped into full view!

The double circus went on for fully five minutes. I could

hardly keep quiet or sit still, it was so exciting. . . . Then an innocent wandering breeze puffed by me. More startling warning could not have been sent those fox parents. Father Reynard, he the smaller, lighter of the two, leaped to the rocky fold beside him, every muscle, every sense taut as a violin string. His nose pointed in my direction. Then away. Then back again. I could see its tip quiver, as his head swung nervously from side to side.

Moments passed, my eyes fixed upon him. I became conscious again of the purring auto stream. . . . In the dusk a screech owl flew soundlessly over my head and alighted in a thorn-apple directly behind the fox. During the instant that my glance was diverted from animal to bird, *the animal disappeared*. No sound, no clue.— And where were the other five? All had vanished! . . .

Walking to the rock and searching in circles around it, I discovered at last a burrow like a woodchuck's. Only a single soiled white chicken-feather gave away the secret.— Now what passer-by would suspect that this burrow harbored six foxes — or, indeed, that this neglected field held such "animal treasure"!

Nearly every Spring since boyhood I have been searching off and on for a fawn. A newborn fawn lying curled up, silent, motionless on the ground amongst weeds or grass or bushes; not one able to run bouncing after its dam, not one half-grown. These I have seen a few times in my life. But never — until last June — did I find my newborn fawn. It happened as casually, as naturally, as you please. We were hunting for pink lady slippers, wife and I. One moment my gaze was somewhat absently bent upon a low tangle of sweetfern scrub twenty feet distant — not in the least concerned about fawns — or hippogriffs. Next instant of time I realized I was staring straight into the round brown eye of a tiny, curled-up, spotted, russet, helpless fawn.—

ANIMAL INFANTS

The eye had blinked! Not a second's questioning or doubt: there one was lying in the warm sun! After thirty years. Casually, naturally. As though newborn deer were common as mice. . . . I heard a crackle of a distant twig and had an instant's glimpse of the doe in the far background; she lurked as close as she dared. I called my wife over. Instantly she cuddled the mite into her lap; she murmured ecstatic little croonings. The whole incident seemed a fairy story, unreal, yet almost too real. . . .

The fawn did not try to escape, even to stand; exhibited absolutely no show of fear; it lay limp as a handkerchief; it made no sound. It appeared to like caressing. Probably there is in all the world no more lovely a wild child than this!

Knowing of the remarkable mechanism of shoulder, hip, and foot joints in deer, we fell to manipulating the tiny legs in all directions; we all but tied the rear legs into a knot around its neck. It seemed triple-jointed, universal-jointed. It could not stand, or would not. We could not make it *try* to stand by our holding it up. So weak did this fact make it appear that, to judge by domestic animals, this creature was not over forty-eight hours old. Surely it could not stagger away from this sunny nook in the sweet-ferns beside the maple saplings. . . While we admired and petted the foundling an hour passed. I wanted so much to have a friend come here tomorrow to see this thing! We reasoned, well, at least its mother cannot lead it away for a day or so; we will come back at sunrise. . . .

The story ended there, as my companion lifted the warm circlet of dappled brown over to its leafy bed, and we crept away.

Next morning there was no fawn there. Not anywhere on the whole twenty-five acres of overgrown pasture. Where? Who could find it again! — That silence and helplessness was a ruse; instinctive self-defense. No other tactic would do. It *could* walk, of course. After a fashion. For positively it must have been led away, perhaps quite far away, by the doe who came as soon as we had gone out of hearing. She had no means whatever of carrying it, though she might have helped it stagger along from time to time. It could not have *escaped* any enemy at its age, by its puny movements through undergrowth. Mother could have defended it against fox, dog, lynx, eagle, vulture, weasel, likely enough. Not against man. But running away never could have sufficed at all. So instinctively it lay utterly quiet, giving forth very little scent; then feigned utter helplessness.

That was in 1941. We never saw it again — I guess. Though there are some fifteen white-tailed deer in the woods just behind my house, and we see a few of them about every day now. . . .

Chipmunks have an unusual way of bringing up children. They keep them strictly at home, apparently all the time underground till they reach an age roughly approximating first year of High School. The thin shy little stripers who are born sometime in mid-March, in these parts, in a dry and remarkably tidy little den two feet down, are almost never seen before the end of April. On their first essays into daylight, the three or four of them stick so closely to the hole in the dirt that they can bolt into it on the least alarm.

Last October we used to watch a Chipso excavate a hole squarely in the middle of the front lawn. The digger brought all dirt up in its mouth, carried it off and left no telltale crumbs at the burrow mouth. We saw him or her provision it for Winter prodigiously with endless successions of bulging cheek-pouches, and also carry in dry-leaf bedding enough to indicate roughly what sized caverns, measureless to man, were being eroded down there (though only one individual winters in a den). Came February, and the first timid warm worning (14°) brought the chipmunk up to skip about on two feet of crusted snow. It is during these first appearances that breeding takes place in the clan, then they more or less completely disappear for three or four weeks. At the end of which time the litters are probably born. But the young seemingly never get out of doors much before May. At that burrow hole in the lawn one early morning the binoculars revealed four gangling two-thirds-grown youths come forth and sit there in a ring, gawky and dumb as halfwits at a fair. Maybe this was their first sunlight. . . . Still gazing at this innocent spectacle, made very intimate by the might of an eight-power glass, I saw mother's nose appear, and she sat among the four. Suddenly a hungering robin dropped to the sod nearby with a braking flash of wings — and utter panic ensued. Bumping noses, crashing foreheads, all five tried to dash into the 1½-inch hole at the same instant. Hardly anything more ludicrous could be imagined. That traffic crush was straightened out in five seconds, yet it *seemed* a long while they tussled to get out of sight. Not until next day did I detect any young chipmunks in the open again.— But so very soon they grew up — that is, as much as any adult chipmunk ever does grow up. By another month they all had staked out claims of their own roundabout and began to mine, hoard, look innocently cunning and not at all rat-like, after the manner of their kind.

Despite the guidance of this thing called Instinct, family ways sometimes get tangled. I recall two instances when litters of Red Squirrels appeared at entirely the wrong season. How or why such a mischance, I do not understand. On the last day of September 1930, we had been felling some old apple trees and were starting to cut up one of

the largest limbs, when a small head startlingly appeared
at a knothole near the saw-cut. A Red Squirrel, full-grown,
shot scolding from the hole and bounded off through the
orchard. Then another face filled the opening, and this too
was shortly followed by body and tail of — a very young
squirrel. On the ground it had no idea what to do; after
a moment of scrambling it was caught under a hat.— A
two-week-old squirrel at the end of September — tragic
misfit! And then there followed no less than six more helpless brothers and sisters. Cold weather and squirrel harvest
time right at hand, and these babies quite incapable of
coping with life.— So I supposed.

In a large open cage outdoors they thrived through Fall
and Winter. We saved their lives — so we assumed — but
did we tame them? Not in the least. I *never* have been able
to *tame* a Red Squirrel. The following April they bit at my
fingers as savagely as ever, and when released merely flicked
their several contemptuous tails and shot off to the woods
forever.

Now it happens that last Fall an almost identical experience befell me. On October 1st, it being at about eight
of the sundial, down the stone walk which leads from
kitchen to woods a hundred feet distant came a procession,
a slow and somewhat sober one for squirrels: four youngsters in red wearing the mien and shape of kindergarten
Red Squirrels. No adults. Just the four — going *somewhere*.
Well, I thought, this is a coincidence! I did not show
myself but followed them at a distance. They went out
to the roadway, up along it to the highroad, and then on
and on. Going somewhere. I never did learn *where*. I've
now changed my mind. I now believe that these callow
specimens of a race renowned for hardihood and independence, *are* able, given a reasonable break in weather
conditions, to survive! I never read or heard of similar

untimely litters, but guess that occasionally this second-litter accident happens, and that the little Reds do pull through — at least sometimes. It's only a guess.

Immediately around the house from two to four families of young Gray Squirrels are raised every Spring. The tree cavities are all within sight from the porch. They are most beautiful children — and most dutiful. When half grown they spend quiet dawns and fading evenings silently running and swinging about on the tree limbs near the nest hole. This they do for exercise and experience, apparently. They almost never stop moving for an hour at a time, if they are not startled. But disappear in a flash if anything appears below. As they get larger the home cavity seems to get smaller, and nearly all litters are taken back to the deep woods at a comparatively early age; probably to occupy a nest of leafage in a tree top. And it is an alluring sight to watch the deftness by which Mother Gray brings it about.

None of the young have by then set foot upon the earth or left the home tree. The adult has to cajole them — contrary to all her previous injunctions — to follow her down, round and round the trunk to the ground. She may get one, or two, upon the turf, only to have them race back in panic as she is working upon another. They seem to find the touch of the earth strange and fearsome at first. But at length she has them all at the tree's foot and gets them to walk after her up to the nearest trees in the woods — and the family all work into the shadows and are gone. Such is the technique for offspring too large to carry. But I have often *seen* her carry the younger size — not in her mouth; I have never seen that, but suspect it does occur with the very immature who must for some reason be moved — and she carries them as a monkey mother transports her child in the jungle: the child clinging around neck, under front legs, and with its own rear feet tight in the fur along the adult's

flanks. Especially is it notable how obedient they are
to parental orders. Life often depends on the habits of sly-
ness and patience which so characterize wild Gray Squirrels.
The young seem always to obey — yet this obedience is
often daintily tempered with shyness, childlike fearfulness.
Life, the world, all is so new! So bewildering! . . .

A baby porcupine is very rarely seen; few citizens *have*
seen one. These wood-eating rodents never stray far from
a rocky den or hollow tree in deep woods, and there one
must go, braving black-fly and mosquito, so much as to
hope to see a family, a trinity, as it were, for one offspring
is about the best a pair can be expected to produce. One
May day I came upon a trio deep in the tangle of a Catskill
spruce slash. The two cowardly(?) adults shuffled off into
utter inaccessibility; the seven-inch infant tried to reach
a hole under a stump but failed because my shoe got into
it first. Whereupon he turned and flowed along over the
forest floor not unlike a millipede worm. Such a feeble,
unmammalian, larval-looking thing! A sort of land-mollusc.
Feet and nose not visible; each end seemingly identical,
seemingly he could proceed with equal ease in either direction.— "Looks like the top of our old cream freezer!"
squealed daughter behind me.— Just that. A push-me-pull-
you with a head at each end. While handling him no
needles stuck into our hands. He had none yet. His pelt was
a coat of bristles; embryonic quills. So flabby and spirit-
less was he that making a pet of him seemed a foolish
objective. Into a crevice he drifted and was gone; I have
never seen his like again.— But I hope to, and maybe next
Spring I will.

Simple Molly Cottontail has a certain flair for mothering — I do not allude to her mastery of multiplication, necessary as that is in counteracting the high mortality rate.
She is not so simple in one respect at least.

ANIMAL INFANTS

My house sits in two acres of cleared land: lawns, gardens, shrubbery. This area is enclosed by a large tract of woods harboring Cottontails galore. Now when Molly and her sisters are to deliver young, invariably they slip out from the woodlands and underbrush and come to our cleared site to make "nests." Cunning nests. A clever habit. Done to evade the several enemies which haunt the woods: Foxes, weasels, skunks, blacksnakes, dogs, raccoons. Molly slyly steals out into the dusk of some April evening, digs a shallow pit beside a grass tussock, lines it with fur tufts pulled from her undersides. There her four to six babies lie, blind, utterly helpless, mouse-colored. Only once in every twelve hours does she visit that spot to nurse them; at dark and before sunrise. Almost never do we see her come or go. During daylight she lies in heavy coverts in the forest. After she departs no eye can discern that nest for she deftly covers it with dead leaves and grass; you must lift aside that covering before you come to what cuddles below warmly and dryly protected. Herein the litter lies at least eight days developing size and pelt with amazing rapidity. From this time on the bunnies are capable of fending for themselves; that is, capable enough to forage in the vegetation all about. By now their strength and the determination with which they can squirm away, push through obstacles and vanish are astonishing. Except for the speed and cunning which come with age, they are nearly as self-sufficient as they ever will be. . . . No "lair" could be less protected, yet more effectively inconspicuous. In place of bravery and weapons of offense, the simple rabbit has sheer stealth. For days I have walked by and even across certain of these litters near the house, not guessing they were there until some chance clue gave the game away.

✿   ✿   ✿

NOW THAT WE HAVE TO WALK

(The author has told about the bear cubs of his youth in his book *The Doorway To Nature* p. 174)

AMERICA'S GAMEST GAME BIRD

—I have seen the time when I would go a good way to shoot a "partridge" but I would not have killed, if I could, the one that started out of the vines that cover my rustic porch, as I approached that side of the house one autumn morning. How much of the woods, and of the untamable spirit of wild nature, she brought to my very door!

—JOHN BURROUGHS: *Riverby*

AMERICA'S GAMEST GAME BIRD

A RUSTLE . . . A twitter . . . A winged explosion: BR - R - R - r-r-r-r . . . Clashings of stiff feathers against twigs . . . BANG! BANG! . . . On the other side of the woods — BANG! Over the hill a fainter Bang! . . . Richly colored leaves carpeting the ground, limbs almost bare, air charged with tang and zest, blue sky, hot sun driving the dry leaf-scent up to the nostrils.— The open season for Ruffed Grouse is upon us!

—Sport for hunters. Death for grouse. *More* death, I mean, more per thousand birds; because statistically they are used to dying. Only relatively few individuals have missed it thus far this year.— I will explain presently why. . . .

If a hunter must shoot grouse, he has to know certain of their ways, and if he should be paradoxically a nature "lover," probably he will wish to know other facts about them. If only out of deference to the skill demanded of him as a gunner, he should be aware of just what manner of hardy fowl this is with whom he "matches" wits — as the phrase is. It is obviously a mere euphemism to say *matches:* the bird never kills the man.

Since so many citizens habitually try to shoot grouse, it is necessary that in most states game authorities discover a great deal more about the intimate ways and means of the birds — not to mention that they must also study the citizen's hunting habits and preferences, and then analyze the results. Of late years it has come into the province of many such state bodies not only to protect grouse from being

[*196*]

hopelessly thinned out, but to try to raise them artificially and distribute them where — for hunters — they will do the most good. Grouse, it turns out, are not easy to breed or to raise in captivity.

A short time ago I looked in on one of these State Game Commissions, that of New York at its Albany headquarters. I wanted those investigators who work with them at first-hand to tell me the latest findings about America's finest all-around game-bird. When the visit was over what bulked largest in my mind was this: "The gunning season is the least fatal period in the Ruffed Grouse's year."— Stated differently that remark means that the hunter is found not to be the bird's most devastating enemy. It contends with six predators more deadly than man. The mortality in any one year caused by shotguns is not, it seems, a controlling factor in determining scarcity or abundance of grouse over a given area. As this conclusion ran counter to my own previous ideas on the subject, I was eager to learn the foundations on which it was based.

We have read a good deal about what happened to game of all sorts when the pump-gun, the automatic shotgun, came into general use. The more public spirited, humane or far-sighted of hunters protested its use from the beginning. Were they over alarmed? Probably not, based on general experience since, and on the significant fact that in 1935 the Federal Migratory Bird Act had to forbid the use, against migratory birds, of any shotgun holding more than three shells.— Alas, our grouse are not migratory! They do not come directly, nationally, under the scope of that Act. . . . Shortly after the advent of the pump-gun came the universal automobile. One heard considerable misgiving expressed as to what the ensuing effects would be upon fish and game when motor cars opened all the faraway nooks of wilderness to hunting and angling parties. The

number of hunting and fishing licenses began at once to
multiply by tens and twenties. . . . And here at Albany
the other day they were trying to tell me that against grouse,
at least, gunning did not matter so very much! — Or were
they?

To get the apparent contradiction straightened out (it is
apparent only) we have to bear in mind several pertinent
facts. First and foremost, probably nowhere today is the
grouse population as great as two decades ago; for it was
then, relatively at their very beginning, that gun and car
lowered the game population markedly all over the East.
Presently, for grouse as for ducks and geese, a dangerous
scarcity loomed; it was now feared that a theoretical dead-
line being reached, the many grouse enemies beside man,
might finish the job; might, assisted by the guns, so nearly
exterminate the bird as to forever prevent it from increasing
again. This fear brought on the innovation of bag limits, a
legal check on individual kills allowed to a hunter, both in
one day and in one season. Likewise a non-legal but cosmic
Law Of Diminishing Returns set in, so that the percentage
of kills to total birds in an area slowly grew less. The fewer
the birds became, of course, the harder to shoot any. . . .
Today in New York three grouse per day is the limit; fifteen
per season. That season is now four weeks long; in the
minds of many conservationists that is yet twice too long.

Before presenting a few details of the Commission's findings as to the destruction wrought by the Ruffed Grouse's
natural enemies, as compared to its human ones, I have
to relate a series of experiences with the birds which fell
to me this past Spring. That series was another reason
which moved me to ask leading questions at Albany.

Within a short distance of my home I found three nests
in early May. Two were but a few hundred feet from the
back porch. Did these birds *seek* man's proximity? If so, is it

because enemies would be found scarcer? — At any rate, several times in the past I have known them to forsake the heart of the woods and nest rather close to homes. Nest One held twelve eggs; Number Two held fourteen; Number Three held an even dozen also. I number them in the order in which I found them during a four-day period. In each case the contents proved to be a full complement of eggs. A week later crows — as I knew from the manner of the despoiling — destroyed all the eggs in Number Two, except one which was cold when I discovered the calamity next morning. Knowing no better, even though I have been familiar with Grouse nests from boyhood, I placed the survivor egg with the twelve in nest Number One, to save at least one chick to the world. Eight days thereafter, on visiting Number One, I found to my chagrin that this one egg had hatched, the dozen had not; and Mother Grouse, true to instinct, had walked off with her one baby and left the rest of her eggs to chill beyond resuscitation.— Which I proved by placing them under a setting hen of mine, to no avail. The mistress of Number Two nest had, it seems, begun incubating before the other mother had — and I had not guessed that!

As for Nest Three: in a day or two more a foraging skunk had eaten every egg. Thirty-eight eggs in three nests marvelously well-concealed, laid by hens which knew how to sit as close at my approach as any I ever flushed, produced one chick. A 2.7 per cent success, a 97.3 per cent failure.— Now, was this an approximately normal expectancy? I could not believe it was, and subsequently learned that it was not. Yet the "normal" expectation of nest-failure, 40 per cent proved dismaying enough. . . . I believe that the average person does not realize how many nests of other birds come to grief. From years of observation in a rich bird habitat, I have reached the conclusion (and several

NOW THAT WE HAVE TO WALK

scientific investigations bear me out) that fifty to sixty of every hundred wild birds' nests have their eggs destroyed in one way and another. Were it not for the fact that most species build a new nest and lay in it within a fortnight, probably few kinds would maintain their numbers. Not so this wild woods hen of ours; the State game authorities told me that unless a Grouse's eggs were destroyed *before* ten days or two weeks from the beginning of incubation, she would rarely lay any more that year. . . .

Walking through a quiet piece of woodland last Memorial Day I was startled by a Grouse suddenly rising about a rod from me with a whirr and fluttering of suspicious violence — more explosive than usual it seemed. The bird flew but a few feet then trailed along the ground, making it at once obvious that she had a brood of chickens which had sunk into invisibility at her warnings. Looking with great care to see that I stepped on nothing but good earth mold, I walked to the big pine stump near where the bird had started up. Standing motionless beside it for several moments, methodically I eyed the nearby forest floor. I could make out no living thing. All at once I became slowly conscious that I had been looking steadily at a tiny brown object below me on the dead leaves, an object which panted. Carefully I stooped and picked up the little fellow and held him for closer inspection. He lay there on my palm, his tiny body rigid, his bright beady eyes as unwinking as if sightless, appearing for all the world like a dark Leghorn chick. During all this time the mother bird, a few rods away, skulked back and forth whining continuously like a puppy, doubtless admonishing the little chaps not to stir foot nor blink eyelid no matter what happened.— Suddenly I saw another chick; then, learning just what to look for, another and another, all lying a short distance from my feet. I made out altogether twelve young grouse-

[200]

lets where an unwarned passer-by would have had no hint
whatever.

I picked up four of the obedient youngsters, and after
admiring them lowered my hand. When within three or
four inches of the ground, quite as if by accident, as a dry
leaf stirs in a barely perceptible zephyr, each rolled stiffly
off and by a slight movement or two shuffled under or close
to some trifling protection. Two hid under my shoe over-
hanging from a root; another slid into a mouse-hole in the
stump; a third burrowed down a trifle into the leaves — and
all was still. . . .

Sitting there on the pine stump I marvelled at this instinctive performance. What, O Knower Of All, does a
Grouse not owe to its forebears! — that at twenty-four
hours of age it should do exactly — not what its mother
warned, but — what the ages told it to do! Birds and animals, I mused, can less afford to pay an inheritance tax
than human beings can, because almost their entire "mental" as well as physical equipment comes down to them,
heirlooms of countless generations. That early instincts of
the very young are able to take care of them before they
have experienced much of the influence of their surroundings, is not to be doubted; here before me that was again
demonstrated. Yet generally we think that most of their
stimuli (causes which make them react in what we term
"instinctive" ways) are recognized and obeyed only after
some extended contact with the world of light and air. We
willingly believe that young things begin life helpless and
with brain and nervous system a blank "white sheet of
paper"— as Dewey puts it — on which life proceeds to write
its memoirs.— If not, just when does instinct begin to act?
May not, indeed, the whole life-in-egg development (on-
togeny) be considered as instinctive; even though it be
commonly called names like physio-chemical *anabolism* or

NOW THAT WE HAVE TO WALK

embryonic growth? Thus viewed, is instinct only another word for total teleology, for *life?* Does instinct merely mean "life, acting"? . . . "Thoughts sublime that pierce the night like stars"— there on the old truncated pine. . . .

When I reached home I remembered to take from my files a yellowed clipping, long treasured. It presented a striking instance of how carefully assembled, delicately adjusted, well-oiled and already running at birth (at the latest) is the machinery of instinct which the wild creature inherits from its race. It was "related by a traveler in South America, a man of scientific repute"— and very likely that traveler was W. H. Hudson, though I know not. He, "the traveler," discovered accidentally the nest of a jaçana in a swamp through which he was riding. He dismounted and picked up an egg to examine.

"All at once the cracked shell parted. At the same moment the young bird leaped from my hand and fell into the water. I am sure the young bird's sudden escape from the shell and my hand was the result of violent effort on its part to free itself. It was doubtless inspired to make the effort by the screaming of the parents, which it heard while in the shell. Stooping to pick it up to save it from perishing, I saw my assistance was not required, for immediately upon striking the water it put out its neck, and with body nearly submerged, like a wounded duck trying to escape observation, it swam rapidly to a mound, and, escaping from the water, concealed itself in the grass, lying close and perfectly motionless like a young plover."

As this sounds to my ear very much like the distinguished style of Mr. Hudson, I am disposed to concede that it does come from "a man of scientific repute." If the incident be

correctly reported, the whole behavior here looks like the
free gift of heredity — then where is John Dewey's "white
sheet of paper?"

         ❉   ❉   ❉

Now to get back to that Ruffed Grouse "Project" which
I knew the State experimenter had been engaged upon
for the past dozen years. The results of one careful check
covering 1030 nests, and another check more recently,
were that about forty per cent were broken up, mostly by
predators. The deadliest egg destroyers proved to be foxes,
weasels, skunks, raccoons, crows, in that order. Also, the
nests, to the extent of thirteen, underwent complete
elimination by forest fire or flood water; twenty-nine were
"broken up by man."— Well and good — rather, bad and
worse — let us see how the chicks fared which did hatch
and leave the nests. To the best of the knowledge of those
who conducted the investigation, annual average infant
mortality to September 1st ran from fifty to eighty per cent,
i. e. always more than half. Take a half from about a half
and you get a quarter; one quarter of the eggs laid were
credited with turning out birds that might be termed adults
for Fall shooting. But to the Spring's eggs and chicks that
succumbed, has to be added a *normal* (exclusive of hunting) mortality among *adults* of from twenty-five to fifty
per cent. That is to say, expectably up to half the breeding
stock met death in a year.— Where does the shotgun come
in on these figures? A series of eight check-areas established
in one well-hunted county, with sportsmen cooperating in
reporting their kills, and a three-year survey resulted in the
conclusion that around fifteen per cent of the birds counted
just previous to hunting season were bagged. Later experiments indicate this fraction to be a reasonable average for
the State at large.

[*203*]

NOW THAT WE HAVE TO WALK

Next comes this matter of "cycles" in Grouse scarcity. A few years back it was generally thought that some mysterious disease ran its course at regular intervals and swept the country almost clean of the birds. This particular cause is under serious question now by those who have good grounds for doubt. While there is general agreement that a cycle of scarcity does come around pretty regularly every ten years, little scientific evidence points to widespread disease. Rather, the matter may be one of recurrent plenty and rareness of mice or rabbits, for the most devastating predators of Grouse are also heavy consumers of both these rodents; their abundance naturally making for less slaughter of Grouse and their eggs.... An official Report on the "Project" issued in 1932 read: "A study of Grouse abundance in this State indicates that 1927, 1917, 1907 and 1897 represented periods of comparative scarcity. And fairly accurate records are available to prove that in 1867 Grouse were also scarce in many parts of the State. Attempts are being made to correlate the occurrence of these cycles with weather conditions, with the abundance and scarcity of species predatory on the Grouse, and with the abundance of rabbits and mice." Some of the cycles, by the way, are found to be somewhat local, others more general in the Northeast. There is a complete survey of all known information obtainable about wild and propagated Ruffed Grouse, and it will be worth obtaining from the Conservation Department of the State by those interested.

The effects of inbreeding on the stamina and therefore the relative numbers of Grouse in a region had formerly considerable vogue as explaining the "cycle." Now we are assured that little if any inbreeding really occurs, because the birds wander so widely from woodland to woodland. And on this matter of breeding, some other findings will interest us. Grouse are not so polygamous as was formerly

[204]

believed. As a strictly fixed habit in the wilds they may rarely mate thus. At all events, censusing the two sexes has repeatedly shown that males slightly outnumber females — as in most species of wild birds. In experiments with artificial raising of grouse on game farms, the State officials discover that wide variation exists in the fertility of females and in sex aggressiveness of males, as also in the fertility of the males. This as yet inexplicable thing persists whether the breeding stock is from wild eggs or those laid by birds in captivity. Polygamy is common to populations living in the wilds. Wild cocks are known to fight one another fiercely at courting time; this may eventuate in one male here and there becoming cock-of-the-walk so far as his range goes, and thus making polygamy the rule thereabout. Captive cocks incline to a surprisingly brief breeding period, thus leading one to imagine that many in a wild state might not be virile enough after two or three years to claim a mate, leaving the field open for the sturdier male to collect a group of wives. In short, the question of virility in wild birds is still being investigated as is the whole puzzling topic.

Ruffed Grouse are probably one of the hardiest creatures which hunters shoot at today. Hardiest under weather conditions, I mean, and as adults. Chicks are not so tough. Grownup, deep snow does not daunt them; always there are buds to be picked off above the deepest drifts; and, putting on a pair of efficient snowshoes of bristles late in the Autumn, they go out into the snow and stay out. Should the nights threaten to be a bit more frigid than usual, they dive full-tilt into a drift to sleep under its insulating warmth. However, holed-in like this, they are easily caught by fox and lynx, and by man too. With snowshoes, food, warmth and wind-resistant feathers, what more do they need! . . . Two hours after hatching as babies they follow mother as lively as crickets over the roughest terrain. In two weeks they fly well enough to escape all human efforts at capture. And that drumming performed by the cocks? Watch it repeatedly. If you are as lucky as I have been in seeing it it is probable you would shrink from swearing in court as to just how they perform it. Country-store debaters up in these parts still hold forth to this day in a three-sided argument about it. Do the birds drum against their own inflated chests? Or against the log or rock they are standing on? Or are they only fanning the air with quick violent strokes? I am inclined to stand with the scientists on the last contention — yet at times have uneasy doubts. In any case, no one is entitled to any opinion until he sees the thing done. . . .

Out at the game-farm as I stood beside one of the breeding pens in which scientists of the State are trying to propagate Grouse — inside it five full-grown hens, sleek, agile, tame; beauties they were! — I asked the overseer innocently: "How many grouse did the State liberate last year?"—"Not any," he answered, "and it never did until this year."

(That was in 1941) "Recently we freed sixty-five birds, under special conditions where we could try and check up on them for some time." (In late 1942 they intend to release a comparable number.) . . .

Later I was quizzing a Department official "at the top": "Tell me, will grouse hold their own much longer in this State with something over 600,000 licensed hunters?" (He had just been telling me that it was officially reported that in 1939, 157,151 were shot in the commonwealth of New York.)

He grinned at my earnestness. "Sure, they will hold their own. In this State the Legislature must see to it, if we can't. Should artificial breeding and distribution prove impracticable, the open season can be shortened and possibly a bounty paid on foxes, weasels, and possibly one other predator — though I have about come to the conclusion that killing off predators on any species, bird or animal, anywhere, is in the long run exceedingly poor conservation, so closely knit is this baffling altogetherness called ecology. Touch one thread, a dozen others start unraveling. The birds have extraordinary staying-powers; they wax and they wane but have never died out, even in the days when there were far more cleared land and cultivated acres throughout this State. Every year more deserted farmland goes back to nature.— Oh, yes, the grouse will be here drumming long after you and I are gone."

Afterward I looked it up: In New York, the most densely peopled State, over two and a half million acres in forest preserve; 450,000 in reforestation areas; and some 100,000 in game-refuges; all public property under some kind of control or management in behalf of wild life. More lands being acquired annually. And this wilderness renaissance is going on by leaps and bounds all over the nation east of the Mississippi; the home now and likely enough forever, of *Bonasa umbellus* — the feathered bombshell you so often shoot at and do not hit!

Daily Bread

Among the aisles of spruce and pine
I planted years ago
I set a table for the birds
who come South with the snow,
here fended from the uttermost
that Winter can bestow.

While cold bites deep and drifts build up,
the board from Fall to Spring
is crowded 'round by trenchermen
as bold in heart as light of wing,
—and neither they nor I believe
the cost is anything.

Perhaps they do not understand,
my transients as they dine,
why suet grows upon the spruce
and grain beneath the pine,
—I too am just as mystified
about this life of mine. . . .

When my frayed wings one day shall trend,
lone migrant flying blind,
southward, southward; at the end
in some Assisi may I find
(where solemn cypress ranks will stand)
a host to humankind.

CHAPTER XVII

WILD LANGUAGE

THE FIELD of intercommunication among animals and birds is one too little explored as yet. It is rank with hokum and nonsense, hearsay and anthropomorphism. As a specialty for one who likes to mix common sense, curiosity, patience and science, there is a lifetime of absorbing investigation here. The compilation of some key generalizations in it, the ratings of some basic psychology inherent in animal mentality and its expression, ought to be worth a doctorate in any man's country. Better still, it should yield a person no end of stimulation and satisfaction. . . .

On a recent October night I was waked by the barking of a fox in the woods behind the house. The bare fact is not noteworthy, however certain circumstances linked with it make it stand out in my experience as a peculiarly poignant memory.

I have lived for several years near a three-mile-long forest tract which edges up toward my back door; "gray" foxes are common hereabout but not the red species. In former years and at various places I have often listened to fox barkings, yelpings and growlings; their noises are well known to me and I could not mistake their identity nor fail to mark a peculiar note if I heard it.

The performance was repeated, now at a different spot. Again after a pause of minutes the fox gave six barks in quick succession at another position. The puplike, asthmatic voice seemed to carry an oddly distracted, worried quality, and it was louder than common, as if calling or signalling to another fox. From time to time came several different series of outbursts, each consisting of some five or six barks, the final one so far distant it could hardly be heard. The fox was covering a wide area and traveling swiftly between calls. That manner of yelping was new to me; even in mating season when a great deal of excitement prevails I had never heard its like.—And, of course, October is not mating time. Autumn outbursts of barking I attribute mainly to parents weaning and hounding out of the neighborhood their young of the year; early Spring or late Winter commotion is practically certain to be concerned with rivalries and courtships.

As I lay there in bed suddenly an explanation occurred to me: I remembered that about noon a hunter had shot a dog-fox half a mile from my home, the first, and it proved later, the only one killed near-by during that gunning season — the period of vulgar and loathsome barbarity! (— That every hunter I know should go into the mystery, magic and serenity of those woods *only once a year, and then only to kill!*) Yes, that fox barking out there in the woods was almost certainly the victim's mate. Sensing something to be wrong because of his non-appearance at the den that night, she had set out to locate him.

Now would that be wholly strange? Mating for a lifetime as they do usually, adult foxes should develop a true affection for one another; at least, come to depend on one another somewhat, become used to living together so that the disappearance of a mate were something of a family calamity. And why might that not cause anxiety to such sensitive, intelligent creatures as these? Dog lovers know that worry and upset are common among canines, at times developing almost to hysteria. — Mind you, I am not suggesting that any human concept of death or injury entered her animal head, but that an anxiety did sound very plainly in her calls. A sequel to this incident two evenings later supported my theory; this time while I was walking across some pastures in the moonlight through a different section of the neighborhood. The same voice, the same distracted quality about it, barking several times at intervals from over a wide area. She was still seeking! Beneath the sound was an emotion a man could not fail to recognize. Here was speech rising straight out of the emotions; communicating no message, but evidencing a "state of mind" (really, a *physical* state) in the speaker. . . .

The plight of the little vixen, my bereft neighbor, led me into a line of thought about the languages of the so-called *lower* animals in general. (How much *lower* they are than ourselves has become doubtful since this War II started!) Is it not a disconcerting fact that ever-better means of international communication do *not* add to mutual trust and understanding, as used to be confidently predicted? Across seas our rational minds meet readily; science and philosophy pass freely. But upon material levels we clash; on tribal, emotional matters we conflict; we get on no better among ourselves than did the Piltdowns and the Cro-Magnons. Obviously, we have been putting too much weight on mere communication. As a matter of blunt truth, we do not always *mean* goodwill. Armaments pile up as a fixed basic policy among nations; schemes of trade conquest lurk secretly in our several minds. Perhaps what is needed is to *feel* nobler impulses and *show* them, rather than to use quicker easier ways of sending wordy messages. Clearly, we peoples understand one another only too well on the age old bases of struggle and competition; we would get on better if we meant what we said. — Just as animals communicate only what they *feel*. Or, putting it differently, feel what they say.

Renowned comedians have often been quoted to the effect that "it's not so much what you say, it's the way you say it."—And so have orators. The hackneyed phrase

NOW THAT WE HAVE TO WALK

seems to be in general the truth. It is a trick of the voice, an effect *from the whole personality*, that puts an act across. The knack of successful funnymen and orators is to reach down deftly, suddenly, into the substratum of a listener's mind where lie so many bits of intuition, vestiges of instinct, childhood concepts, scraps of racial wisdom, scattered pieces of emotional junk: prejudices, malices, lusts, tendernesses, egotisms, patriotic tag-ends; all never till that second put coherently together "in so many words," and to utter the unsaid for him. They touch his unconscious where the pre-cultural stuff common to all humanity is buried, and in a flash awake subtle mutual understanding, evoke direct, *uncalculating* response. Rather than the give and take of reason and facts, such people communicate their own emotional slant to the more timid drift of their hearers. Thus, as the saying is, they dominate the feelings of their audience. Hitler's inherent brutality and hysteria undoubtedly take possession, temporarily at least, of all his listeners not *mentally* equipped to withstand them. . . . In so far, human mass response resembles the result of animal languages. But animal language cannot go further. Since animal life has no writing, no science, no abstract or complex "ideas" to transmit, its "talk" consists of the sparse vocabulary of impulse, feelings and action.

Every keen observer of outdoor nature should recognize this. Yet I am aware that writers among us seldom draw a human analogy to the fact. Because we are mammals first and man-animals second, talk came late to the apes, therefore much of our conversational vocabulary is not yet in the dictionaries. Much human chat-ter is essentially animal-like — and this is not meant as a cheap witticism. Let us see . . . Did you ever notice that most of those with whom you converse use a few monosyllabic noises again and again for covering a whole gamut of responses? "Yeah?" . . .

"No?" . . . "Swell" . . . "Ah" . . . "Oh" . . . "Well" . . . etc.
It works! Germans utter "So-o-o," Spaniards "Si," in a score
of significant inflections, with a drawl, facial expression,
intonation, to match. The American "damn" "assumes all
shapes from Mah to Mahi" in reporting anger, delight, dis-
gust, sorrow, — every conceivable shade of meaning. — Of
exactly such stuff is animal language comprised.

Ordinary "everyday conversation" demands few words;
subtlety of vocabulary can be dispensed with as it is between animals. The recent scheme, "Basic English," enables a foreigner mastering 850 words to get about readily
and feel conversationally at home. Wider vocabulary is
strictly needed only for dealing with abstractions, *i. e.*
ideas. Street Americanese hardly resembles the tongue in
which we discuss science or write books. Chinese spoken
language is quite incommensurate with the written one.
Probably few intelligentsia in the world use literary style
when excited or under arrest.

If animal beings never exchange ideas nor indeed have
them, what then do they communicate? Emotions usually.
Sudden impulses. Calls to action. Stray acts of caution and
warning learned directly from vivid sense reactions in the
past. When mother fox "teaches" her kits about traps or
makes them distinguish between harm and not-harm, she
is not transmitting the general concept like "hunter" or
"trap"; but is directing an instinctive fox-wariness in them
toward something which has impressed itself on her
physically, something by which through pain or discomfort
she has escaped death. In some way she is capable of
"conditioning" them against an object she is wary of. Her
words are few and straight to the point.

We are told that one uses in general only as many words
as are *needed* to make oneself understood among his group;
the average citizen here seems to possess less than 15,000

speakable words – though he will recognize others in print. Animal vocabularies are very small because the *need* is meager. Yet all organisms even the "lowest," may have something to "say," and where it is not audible or visual, it arises from touch or scent, as among the insects and classes below. There appear to be but two absolutely dumb mammals: giraffe and kangaroo; they are known to communicate by tail and ear movements and by the panic of flight. Such indifferent conversationalists as 'possums, skunks and porcupines can be heard to *mumble* at times; it was only after many years of familiarity with skunks that I *heard* them. – Two adults and four youngsters contending over a plate of soupbones under my bedroom window, produced an assortment of muffled squeals, grunts, squeaks and growls, the like of which no book on skunks which I had read gave me any notion.... Bats signal sometimes in vocal sounds too high-pitched for human ears, sometimes as audible as the squeakings of mice; my dog has shown me he hears them when I do not. Francis Galton, famous English biologist proved by experiments with shrill whistles that dogs could detect notes well above the range of man's hearing.

When one comes to Crows, always alert and noisy, one finds a rare zest in living and a wide variety of ways of expressing it; they make a greater number of sounds than any other wild bird. One Spring I kept a crude record of the different calls I could distinguish. It ran to ten. I am sure that since then I have heard at least two more. Many will be recognized, after some practice, as definitely indicating moods and meanings. Frank M. Chapman wrote: "No one who has listened to Crows will doubt they have a language. But who can translate it?".... Hardy, inquisitive, omnivorous, heavily beaked, strong footed, their kind inhabit the whole earth. Equipped by nature to be, as one might say, the Highest Common Denominator among birds, they cooperate, live long, are wise, and have much to say to one another. Egged on by a nation-wide tradition that crows can easily be taught to speak, country boys covet them as pets. Tradition further holds that for the miracle to occur, the bird's tongue must be slit in infancy. As a boy I raised one — tongue not slit — and several were at various times in possession of my young friends — tongues sometimes slit, sometimes not — and to settle a skepticism encountered nowadays, I can testify that 1. they can be taught to utter words and sounds; 2. they seem to have a more flexible vocal power with the tendon under the tongue slit; 3. the seemingly high intelligence of some of them is uncanny, even upsetting to certain theories on the character of animal mind; and 4. they develop, along in their second year especially, into the highest grade nuisance there is. . . . But, after all, their "language" as pets is simply parrot language— no more.

Long observation among them leads me to conclude that wild creatures have only eight basic needs for language.

The *danger-signal* reason. This is the universal dialect, the *lingua franca* understood between most birds and mammals. — Sometimes it springs from fear, oftener, I think, actual fear must be lacking at the moment of utterance, the signal being automatic with flight. Woodchuck's powerful whistle or chipmunk's sharp chirp, as they dive for safety to sit waiting just below ground, puts the whole nearby fauna on the alert. The chinkling buzz of the Red Squirrel or Gray's scolding barks are the bane of deer hunters. Once in the Adirondack foothills, unseen, unscented for half an hour, I had watched a pair of Red Foxes at courting antics. Suddenly a passing jay spied me and hardly had emitted two screams before up went the foxes' ears and noses, they looked cautiously about, and disappeared. Sight unseen. They took the jay's tip. On another occasion, a single slap of a tail on the water caused the immediate submersion of a whole colony of beavers working on a dam near me. A rabbit's stamp on the ground is a warning signal.

The *keep-together* reason, important to groups and families, especially when migrating or hunting. Expressions for this purpose employ not only calls but also flight-marks, conspicuous flashings of feathers or furry tails that can be seen afar. Such marks serve as warnings also. A Ruffed Grouse's wing-beats when startled create an explosion of sound which carries to its scattered associates both warning and a come-along-with-me-this-way message. At times the keep-together signal takes on the aspect of mutual encouragement, as among migrating geese, which, in plain sight of each other in the sky, will steadily honk, honk along as though chanting away weariness. — Just as do Chinese coolies engaged in an especially tough piece of carrying, say of a grand piano or a 250 pound pig.

There are also to be communicated *mating excitements;* the *distress notes* of hunger or pain; the sense of overflowing *jubilation and well-being;* expressions of parental *affection* uttered near nest or young; the overflow of hot emotion during *combats* or *angry preliminaries;* and, finally, *hunting cries* emitted by predatory animals and by hawks and owls, apparently intended to send prey scurrying to cover and revealing its whereabouts. Concerning hunting cries, I have often been asked (especially back in the days when that rousing tale "The Voice of Bugle Ann" was popular) — and asked myself — why a single hound or a pack bays while hunting. My guess is that, although baying does keep a pack together and following the leading trailers (in whom the others place confidence) the most important end accomplished by the din is the agitation, nervous tense-ness and "worry" of the victim; a body-state which costs it definite physical strain and quicker exhaustion. — It is a canine counterpart for the "human" War-of-Nerves we know so much about of late. — An objective, by the way, probably coming out of an *evolutionary* process, not a conscious calculation on the part of the bayers. — Though I admit being at loss to understand just how it could *evolve* into a species habit.

A widely accepted modern theory to account for most bird-song holds that a male sings to advertise his pre-emption of an area as his nesting and feeding site; that thereby he attracts females to it, and that he stands ready to drive away competing members of his species. I am sure we have to add this as the ninth of the above list of communication purposes, for it is in large degree the motive behind singing. But it is very closely akin to sheer healthy, lively jubilation, even around the home-site (just as ours is!), and such jubilant well-being surely more truly explains what occurs when, for instance, a whole tree in Spring is filled with Goldfinches singing in the mass for hours and hours. — Or what is behind the glorious singings of Purple Finch and Rose-breasted Grosbeak on their migrations towards their nesting areas. We behold "flight-songs" in mating times of such birds as the Northern Yellowthroat, the Woodcock, the Indigo Bunting, that express only ecstasy and delight — that is obvious.

Human we are and humanly we must reason. — When you hear half the small birds of the neighborhood making a tremendous racket, each after its fashion, one need be no linguist to conjecture the presence in the offing of cat, snake, jay, owl, Red Squirrel or hawk; a creature's warning cries need no interpreter either for man or for animals of differing species. — Yet it is not easy to determine just what a North Woods porcupine is driving at at two A.M.

[*217*]

when it comes tottering into your tent, snuffling feebly and testily, "Dear, dear, dear!"— But probably Mrs. Porcupine knows. And all his relatives. Perhaps too the Creator knows, for He alone originated porcupines in the first place. I never heard this quilled brother utter warning calls of any sort. Yet, after all, it is not in the need of things that lower orders should hold converse with noble humanity, nor vice versa, though some of us nurse a sneaking hanker to "listen in" on nature whenever we can. . . .

Among mammals, whose welfare is more dependent on stealth than that of most birds, sign-language is the commonest communication. — How various is the use of a tail! What cannot a dog say to us with it! The Gray Squirrel clinging to a trunk and brandishing his caudal appendage says: "Watch out, something queer here!" Deer, antelope, rabbits when they dash away show the white flag normally concealed on the tail's underside; silently it proclaims: "Here, out here, out this way!" Domesticated cattle, thoroughly startled, or alarmed by odor of carrion or blood, raise tails high in the air like wild things and go dashing about. The feline family, including household pussy, display several types of emotion tailfully and without a sound. Animal eyes being mostly incapable of varying their expression, the ears usurp this function; riding horses and circus elephants thus let trainers know when they feel out of sorts.

I have discovered that my city visitors are much more aware of one outdoor sound than we countryfolk. We are too used to it to hear it without consciously directing our attention. I refer to the dense, constant pulsation of insect calls during Summer and Fall. This underlies all acute noises out of doors. It is conceivable that a stranger from the Arctic might find that steady undercurrent distracting. It is a true Earth Song; a sort of natural Bolero; incessant, maddeningly monotonous if you concentrate on it. Milliards of crickets, locusts, grasshoppers fifing, whirring, clicking, purring among the grass-roots twenty-four hours on end; crescendo, crescendo as the weeks go by and numbers increase; rolling up aggregate bels and decibels of sound! And upon it all, at nightfall in Autumn, katydids pour out veritable torrents of raucous argument. . . . And all this for what purpose? Well, love-lures and exuberance. All this while they little realize that it is later than they think; so short a life of joy and love is theirs! Hardly one among billions will survive the Winter. Yet, they somehow are glad that life is good, and love, though fleeting, is the chief end of life. As of man.

In the daytime, adding to the chorus higher in the air, bees, wasps, beetles, cicadas, are all broadcasting vibrations at various frequencies. By vibration changes perhaps they indicate — yes, even *emotions* of some queer sort, to whose narrow ranges up and down our ears are probably tone-deaf. A practiced apiarist readily distinguishes the anger-buzz from the contented hum of bees-at-work. When swarming is taking place among my hives, the new humming is detectable at once and from a distance. . . . If you wish to study more intently the simple language of insects, you have but to cage them. There is hardly a more intriguing experiment than stocking little cricket-cages with the several insects species. You may watch and listen to your heart's content, and find out how the divers sound mechanisms operate. A few morsels of food, a few cubic centimeters of air, a few ounces of earth — and the world is theirs, sufficient unto the day. . . .

> "He that hath ears to hear, let him hear . . .
> Day unto day uttereth speech,
> and night unto night sheweth knowledge" . . .

Hills like These

Together we watched the darkened hills
Fall softly into the arms of the night.
And we were moved by their friendliness,
Their warmth. We thought of hills like these
Rocked and torn by bombs, earth which knew
The gentle flow of rain, soaked in the heaviness of blood.
We thought of sleeping hills
Where lovers walked, made vows, and dreamed.
Hope — hope never dies, but how were we
To know that a year from now, or even a month,
And I too may have gone where the warm earth
Heaves and pounds under the deadliness of war?
We clasped our hands firmly; if the sacrifice
Is ours, we will keep the gladness in our hearts
Knowing that we shall have given that others
May walk these hills, and dream, and build!

—LANSING CHRISTMAN

CHAPTER XVIII

DAMON AND PYTHIAS

LONG ago, as everyone knows, a certain Pythias willingly
offered to forfeit his life to save that of his friend Damon
whom Dionysius the Tyrant of Sicily — in quite the modern
manner — had condemned to die for protesting against the
tyranny. Touched by such utter fidelity, the despot par-
doned the one and publicly praised both of them for their
fidelity. — Wherefore the names as symbols have lived on
ever since in song and story.

Up-country here I have a modern version to relate. It
involves game pheasants instead of game men. And it ends
not in immortality but in tragedy. For in 1941 A.D. a young
man native to these parts, a neighbor of mine (and though
he is outwardly adult, surely was "unaware of the nature
and quality of his act," as the statutes phrase it), shot
Damon with one barrel, having missed Pythias with the
other. — A fate strange indeed for a life-partnership lived
in simple Spartan hardihood! — A tragic reward to two
beings that never in any way trespassed against man nor
violated any code of nature! . . .

The dual biography begins with the egg — as all life
everywhere does. To human eyes there was nothing about
these shells to distinguish them. They were lying there
with nine others in a nest beneath a ground-hugging,
shoulder-high spruce in my evergreen plantation. Though
diligently sought, this nest never would have been found
had not the sitter hurtled off, a feathered cannonball, at
the instant — and not until that instant — my shoe touched
her side. Nest-and-contents, how perfectly camouflaged!
A Thing merely, an integrated Objective in sunshot brown,

[221]

neutral; the tint of sere grass and leaves underfoot, barred with the shadows of overhead twigs; at one with the ground, matching the piece-goods which earth wears for a northern May Day.

Again on a second day, and on a third, she remained sitting there flattened, motionless, as though hardened like stone, mothering as long as she dared while a friend to whom I unwisely confided the secret came on both those days to photograph the alluring sight. — Alas, upon the fourth day he found the olive-tinted eggs cold. A deserted nest! — Even bravery has its limits, as many a bird and animal seem to know.

Nothing to do but to take the eggs home and place them beneath a broody hen, hoping that the incubation process had not wholly stopped ... A fortnight elapsed and in due course transpired that commonplace miracle of bird faith — life out of stone shells. But of the eleven eggs two only responded, apparently the two most richly endowed with *élan vital* or spirit or EMF-potential or whatever it is currently named, which brings forth life more abundantly. Only two chicks emerged at last, after hours of feeble pecking and pecking as they rotated slowly within their prisons, trepanning out a section at the large end. After the manner of all their genus they squirmed from the stony placenta damp and quivering. That which was spirit mysteriously moving in the dark became flesh-and-blood vertebrate, now wholly obedient to ultra-violet, vitamin and chlorophyl — a life in the sun, of course no less mysterious than before.

That was on the morning of May 28, 1938. Within two hours the infants were able to scuttle about much more alert and stronger of leg than barnyard chicks. — For all their puny vigor, when they kept wriggling off my palm and falling to the floor hurtlessly as autumn leaves, could I have understood then that these downy ouncelings would in the cycle of time each become seven pounds of energy and splendor; and, linked in some strange compact, walk side by side as brothers? — Expressing an egoism-of-two which marked them from the beginning and set them apart from all pheasants I had ever known. . . .

Thus began the careers of the Ring-necked twins; a long companionship which was only to terminate at the bark of a gun in the hands of a young clerk who — Heaven now forgive him! — knew not what he did.

I brought them up, chick to gangling cockerel, to broiler and to near-adult, in a wire pen removed and quiet — as was their right — by the edge of the spruce plantation which now covers the ten-acre lot behind the barns where grandfather pastured his flocks by night, as his sons did also. Wary, highstrung, these wild foundlings showed almost nothing in common with fowls of the hen-roost. They seemed to require quietness and the soothe and whisper of the woods. Never one sound from them, never once a vulgar scramble to the feed-box. Furtive, observant, shy. Cock-birds they both turned out to be; cocks that during four first months of growing, favored their mother in sober hue and early markings. Never startled or panic-stricken at my approach, they refused to act like pets; rather, it appeared, having no inkling such a sycophant state existed. They maintained a sly, watchful aloofness which exactly resembled complete indifference. When October frosts came they had completed the first moult and began assuming that cloak-of-the-spectrum, that regal rainbow of feathers which is the heritage of the male line of Ring-neck Pheasants stretching back through the centuries to the Caucasus slopes of ancestral Asia — Rajahs among birds.

Then arrived the morning when I opened the wire door of the pen. Magically they were free. At liberty to go and be adult pheasants like their forbears in the Karakorum or

NOW THAT WE HAVE TO WALK

Azurbaijan. An hour previous I had picked them up and carefully fixed upon each the numbered aluminum bands which — one on the right, one on the left — would identify them for a lifetime; chart their wanderings if trapped or if they fell victims to what is so oddly called "sport." No alarm about this banding, no indignity. . I stood watching the beautiful pair while they stepped daintily, cautiously through the barrier which had so long fended from them fox, weasel, cat and hawk; peered here, peered there, and stole slowly along the edge of the evergreens; acting their doubt that the little world which they had but looked at for months was now theirs to explore; a great green world, with mystery, wonder, surprise, karma. The myriad green recesses of the little spruce planting offering invitation and secrecy, the birds took steps with deliberate suspicious slowness. The sun and shade patterns on the ground which they entered, crossed, left, dimned and lightened alternately the colors of their racial regalia. — How exotic those burnished tropical pigments against the dark evergreen background; how unfitted to our tame sober landscape; how impractical amid so many dangers their rich raiment! However, would they not anywhere give the impression of unbelonging? Flaunting such gaudiness, would they not be exotic even in their native Asia? In Mongolia, Turkestan, Tibet, Colchis? Here among our unpretentious wildlife the male suggests a painting, an artist-made creation, a man-bred showpiece rather than the hardy all-weather bird he is? . . .

The two must have been aware of me back there all the time, but they do not seem to see me. They seem to be looking away beyond me — perhaps to the far vistas of life ahead. Now one of the awestruck explorers slides slowly into an aisle of planted spruces and melts from view; now the other. — Shall I see them or know them again? . . .

That first Winter the two stayed together. — No question

[224]

as to identity with those leg-bands. In the garden picking at stray ears left in cornstalk heaps; foraging for bush buds; in times of sleet and deep snows sharing grain thrown out; occasionally flying high over barn and house from feeding-place to feeding-place; they hold the whole plantation as their private preserve. A royal pair. Two young blades side by side. Preferring to remain aloof and in their pride to walk the floors of Winter flashing, glowing as though verily to melt the snow about them.

With Spring's return several pheasants appeared round-about on the premises; females were noticeably multiplied over last year. In all probability pheasant life was going on as usual though bursting foliage and growing grass screened away their affairs from human knowledge. Frequent crow-ing and cackling heard far and wide indicated that the time was come when the two comrades should be stirred by an urge more powerful than the ties of brotherhood; they should be seeking mates — harems, rather. Were they? If so, how was their friendship bearing the strain? Though it had survived the comradely days of adolescence, could it persist into days of maturity and mating? . . .

Then one day there came a vivid demonstration of that conflict between Brotherhood and the Racial Urge. In a later afternoon about the tenth of May a long-continued petulant cackling finally obliged me to slip over to a spot in the meadow beside the willow-lined brook. Guided by the sounds I suddenly find myself peering over into a cocking-main as fierce as it is aboriginal, natural. Human tricks and cunning could not have matched two more equal champions nor goaded them into a greater jealousy. Two gorgeously plumaged cocks are engaged in a conflict ap-parently well-advanced which is wearing them down min-ute by minute; a battle of attrition — not a battle to the death; surely not that. For lacking the savage steel spurs which men attach to their birds, wild birds can rarely kill one another.

The clear light of a setting sun shines squarely upon the scene, strongly illuminates the gold, copper, orange and red and purple brilliance of the fighters, and it keys these colors to their richest intensity. Over and over again with long slender tail-feathers sweeping in graceful wide curves, they leap, strike at one another or fall heavily missing their aim, only to whirl away at once to jockey for new positions of attack. A frenzy of motion, kaleidoscopic, glittering. The mad dance of royal Fire Birds! — Could a Stravinski really set this thing to music; could a Gauguin really paint this scene? — Never could they have seen life and color together more vibrant or more active! Bright yellow of willow branches arching above; green of new meadow grass ringing the arena, the level spotlight of sun striking in. . . .

At times the combatants are forced to stop for a moment, panting, and with open beak and pulsing wings, poised, glaring at one another with bated malevolence and striving for breath to reopen the onslaught. Then a dash, a leap, a whirl too swift to follow, a guttural catch in the throat and the swishing sound of wingfeathers against twig and stalk. . . . For a half hour I watch the battle. So near that I am able to see the aluminum bands upon the fighters' legs. Yet I am unnoticed, or at least ignored; merely a biped restrained from duelling thus for its mate; merely a supplicant to society for its privileges. Yonder is no begging of leave; it is one of nature's primal challenges. This is the way strong hearts and sound bodies and their glorious raiment have prevailed down through the centuries. . . . In the end, as is the way of such struggles for prestige and posterity, one bird (who wears his band upon the right) begins to draw back and hesitate and come in less promptly to the clinches. — Realizing yet hating the knowledge of its defeat. And down along the brook the battle gradually moves out of sight among the willows. . . .

One of my birds established his domain at the south end of the planting, the other at the north, a half-mile distant. — Pythias with the left band, Damon with the right. Each with his own little group of households. — And one of them content with mates and nest-sites perforce of a quality a little short — but a very little short, I hope — of his highest desires. Such is the folk law of Asian nomads; that to the victor belongs the richest spoils, and only to the bravest fall the fairest. Such, more rigidly, must be the code of Asian pheasantry; for, polygamists all, the Ring-neck cock is the Moslem, the warrior, the proud male to his tail-tip; conspicuous and aggressive, a wild abandon and bravura inhere in all his ways. His sex being less given to skulking in stubble and shrubbery, he rises first of the flock when it is startled; flies swifter than the dull-hued hens, and not as far; thereby making himself target of hawk or man; or on foot the quarry to distract the quadruped enemy; ever a potential sacrifice for the female and young upon whom the race most specifically depends. . . . Presently lush Summer closed around the intimate doings of Damon and Pythias — their second Summer. Haying was completed ere our pheasant retainers showed themselves freely again.

Judging from the bitterness of that Spring battle, I naturally concluded that eternal feud had been declared between the blood-brothers. — But no, Summer passed into rich long Autumn, and with Winter stripped and stark again, there were the two birds leagued and inseparable, foraging and flying as though no rift had come between. Out on the white expanses of level meadow a pair of moving dots, through the fresh snow in the plantation aisles two wallowed trails, under the tufted cottony skirts of a spruce two sleepers crouching side by side; near the house in sunny weather twin "Birds of Paradise" with the light of Asia glinting from their breasts, stripped ears of corn and pecked sunflower seeds with an air of unhurried majesty. Their kin and kind, females and young of the year, were left to shift for themselves, disdained, beneath the notice of royalty. This seemed somewhat unnatural. Yet it fits the probabilities that the two actually found their own old renewed companionship a natural, habituated thing, more safe for both than common flocking with the mob.

The contest for mating supremacy in April or May following, if it did take place again, I did not see. However, that Spring three nests were found; the last discovered under dramatic circumstances.

One early morning alarmed cackling from the plantation caused me to investigate, leading me to the very area in the spruces which Damon and Pythias should have been able to recognize as home. The birds heard me coming through the swishing trees and their outcry abruptly stopped. But a few more steps — and I faced a skunk; a full-grown, full-stripe snooper pottering along down a row of saplings in the casual, near-sighted fashion of its kind. We met almost head-on; had I been as near-sighted we probably would. Happily I saw the skunk just in time to sidestep into an adjoining row. Peering through the branches I made out that Mephitis was intent upon something of interest at the base of a little spruce a few feet distant. Its upheld nose was testing the air for a scent it had momentarily lost. The skunk turned toward that spruce, had taken one step, when from another spot among the nearby evergreens darted a bird form in glittering armor; a body fully as large as the skunk and activated by tenfold its dash. Straight into the astonished black-and-white's face, heavy wings trailing, the pheasant cock threw himself and delivered

a series of lightning beak thrusts before the clumsy animal
could assume a position of defense.

Then the bird backed away clucking furiously. But not
far back. At that instant I saw *two* cocks standing there together. — My two protegés, little doubt! Taking stance
between that little spruce and the animal, they intended
to defend a nest hidden right there. Damon also, he whose
band was on the right, was here too and would have died
for Pythias — or Pythias' wife! Rivals, now in common
cause, forgetting rivalry, joined against a greater enemy.

Little Mephitis paused and considered. Evidently it had
now caught the idea — a nestful of juicy eggs over there,
two or three meals of them. Good! What mattered the op-
position of two mere birds, even two cock pheasants, to the
big brother of a weasel? — Yet it stood to consider tactics.
For a few moments the opposing lines faced each other. A
short forward move by the skunk set off another spiteful
charge. But this time the quadruped was not unready; a
front paw in a clutching stroke all-but reached its assail-
ant's head. Perhaps it was magnificent, that battle, but it
was not war. Courage was not enough. A matter of minutes
only before the skunk would be at the eggs. And if not most
wary the cocks themselves might be caught or hurt; those
wicked curved claws were no trifling weapons. Plainly time
had come for reinforcements. I stepped from concealment.
The startled pheasants faded into the undergrowth, and
with a sudden outburst of squawking the setting hen cata-
pulted from the nest. But the furry marauder never batted
an eye; standing ground his little black snout pointing up
at me, not the least notion of flight occurred to him, the
one wild creature men cannot bully at all. Up went the
plumy tail. A warning signal. Seldom does a 170-pound
man disregard that. I retreated. If now I went home for a
rifle, the havoc would be over before I could return; if I

stayed and closed in, I risked a fate worse than death. I also paused and considered. . . Well, I could *call* for help, couldn't I? — Of course. And another man would come with the gun. Little Mephitis couldn't have counted on that. . . The gun, of course, decided the affair. All those pheasant eggs hatched. . .

That Autumn the pheasant clans waxed mightily and prospered, and roundabout there became many. Damon and Pythias drew apart from them again and always together roamed the countryside — a phenomenon unique in my observations and reading. In the Fall and Winter of 1940-41 the plantation became again their preserve; few if any others seemed to venture in. Then we come to last May; it was our luck to see the perennial trial of strength between the rivals. It was no such contest as the first one, however; the fire had gone out of it. Rather it seemed a matter of principle than of principals; a formal ritual of Spring, the result foregone. — If Pythias were Sultan, at all events, Damon was Pasha in the realm. . . .

The fourth year of the Brotherhood drew to its tragic close. High over the house on frosty mornings began again to pass that pair of soaring monoplanes; tails like ailerons, breasts flaunting the colors of the September sunrises. The days were approaching which we dread with a deep visceral dread and a moody resentment: the Hunting Season. Over these acres set aside as sanctuary for every furred and feathered refugee persecuted elsewhere in the name of sport, we are obliged to maintain a relentless vigilance in upholding a printed manifesto pasted thereon in the name of The Law. We keep at bay — if we can — those local "outdoor men" whose interest in outdoors appears to center solely upon two weeks in the year; in which brief period they so dearly love to view the Autumn glories through the sights of a gun.

DAMON AND PYTHIAS

On the day the season opened I heard a shot, and it seemed sickeningly close. Then a second one. I ran over to the plantation. — What had occurred I have already related: Damon had stayed a half-second too long upon the wrong side of the fence, in the No Man's Land of slaughter. The bold Executioner whom I confronted — ah, too late by sixty seconds! — is "a good boy" who works inside the village grocery on all the other weeks of the year, and during all the days of this fortnight except two. Well fed, unmarried, on steady wage, he cannot be said to lack any necessity which a "Bird of Paradise" conceivably might supply. What human end attained by him that day was, I wonder, half so precious as the life he ended. . . .

For a time Pythias walked alone among the well-trodden ways. Then, at length, either he went forth to join the Others beyond the Pale, or the Others came to join him and eventually absorbed him into their lowly routines — who can say? At any rate, the Winter just passed has brought no leg-banded pheasant to the green mansions stretching off behind our place. Pythias could die for Damon, but now not Damon for Pythias; only for himself. — And that, perchance, is exactly what has happened. For there are many other such gunmen in No Man's Land beyond the confines of my posted fences.

Toward God

Oh, erase what you have written about God,
About saints and angels,
About one man being saved and another damned,
About good and evil.

You have tracked a red fox in the snow
Or a deer on the hills of winter,
But who has traced God to his secret place?
Who has lifted the curtain and said, "Behold, He is here"?

The ocean would stagnate and shrink,
The pores of earth would open and receive the rivers of
    the sea,
But the water rises as vapor and returns as rain,
And land and sea are renewed.
Suns and their planets burst into flame and disappear,
But the whirling gas and fire-mist condenses and coheres
And there is life again.

What have the professors, with their microscopes
And telescopes, their retorts and crucibles and tubes,
Their measures and scales, learned about God?
That the core and body and soul of the universe is all life
    and energy,
An aggregation of tiny particles,
Atoms, protons, electrons,
In smaller than microscopic orbits
Spinning around invisible magnetic suns,
That life is everywhere and indestructible — and Life is God.

And life radiates energy,
That is the eternal law,—
Man is vaporized, dissipated, discharged as excrement,
At last reduced to ashes
And blown about like invisible vapors that rise from the sea,
Or gases that escape the vortex of a burning sun.
Yet new life springs Phoenix-like upon the ashes of the old,
New cells cohere and coordinate,—

That is the eternal sequence,—
Life is forever born and God renewed.

God is immanent, not dwelling beyond the stars
Nor in you, but you in God.
And you thought all things were made to minister to your
    needs,
To subserve your every desire —
Oh, foolish man, destroy what you have written about God!

    —William W. Christman: *The Untillable Hills*

CHAPTER XIX

HUMILITY BEFORE BEES

How doth the little busy bee
Improve each shining hour,
And gather honey all the day
From every opening flower !

    —Isaac Watts: *Divine Songs*

If hymn-singing Isaac Watts intended this quatrain as a
question, unanswerable and mysterious, he, back in 1750,
had "nothing on us." We cannot answer such a query, for
we are still guessing. We know *what* bees do — in large part.
Pretty much so did the Greeks, the Egyptians, the Romans;
though a great deal has been learned since. — Also, *why*
they do it is fairly obvious — bees must live. The same as
must Collembola, Mayflies and Poison Ivy. If you do not ask
a *second* Why to that; the *élan vital* or will-to-live answer
stands.

    But *how doth* the busy bee carry on the very best organ-
ized social economy in the world? — of that we know hardly
a jot more than did the Greeks, Egyptians and Romans.

NOW THAT WE HAVE TO WALK

Even in these days when electrons are being photographed and weighed;when we may through a tube study nebulae so far away that their light going 186,000 miles every second takes 100,000,000 years to reach us; even in wonderfully bloody today, men of science are standing only upon the threshold of *bee life*, gazing in wild surmise at works beyond their ken! (—Are they, then, only on the doorstep of *human* life?)

Something there is about bee ways which does not lend itself to measurement; an awe-making something which has not been grappled by the sharpest tools in the laboratory: it is *an awareness*, apparently clairvoyant and superhuman. A power especially of intercommunication, surpassing radio in variety and quality. . . .

Theirs is the oldest civilization known; going back over 100,000,000 years too. Fossil records seem to indicate that it has changed little since then. It operates under a government without an executive head; a communist government, a tribal soviet whose 50,000 and more citizens are offspring of one mother and father. This State is a self-perpetuating system based on a repeating One Year Plan so well calculated, so unimprovable, that it has nothing to learn and nothing to forget. . . .

In the course of a conversation with a young farmer recently I happened to ask if he liked to read detective stories. "They're mostly too unreal," he said. "Too made-up. Now, there's a real one out yonder." He pointed his pipe-stem towards the bee hives. "There's puzzlers in them that I never git tired of. Murders and robb'ries and secret writin' that I couldn't solve if I tried. — 'N I try too, sometimes.". . .

I knew what he meant. I have kept bees. To the wisest among men the hive is an unfinished detective story, a living question-mark, an unexplored country, an "act of God,"

[234]

which moves in mysterious ways its wonders to perform. Yet, amazingly enough, the practical man, the dirt farmer, without need for a *theory* as to the ultimate "how" of the thing he sees, turns the whole process to his advantage. Managed by an equally abstruse mystery, man, the hive inmates become obedient slaves; money-makers, at his command; without being exploited or harmed by their servitude.

Try to explain their actions by a "mechanistic" theory; that is, on a basis of physics and chemistry: you may contend that animals (*i. e.* bees) eat because they are moved by an internal chemical index condition called hunger. Show that some lowly organisms automatically stir toward sunshine or artificial light, some away. Determine that moisture in soil warmed by Spring heat starts seeds to manufacturing their stored starch into sugars and thus begin germinating. Such matters you may safely explain to the credulous as being physico-chemical effects of temperature, humidity, solar radiation, and the like; and that similar "causations" make bees go forth and collect food; decide when they should return at night; set them to sealing cracks in the hive, etc. "Explain" a few other habits mechanistically, perhaps; but beyond a few, ah, there you flounder, groping in abysmal dark.

Never did Maeterlinck, Fabre, Lubbock or Dallas Lore Sharp, describe a bee observation more movingly than has Wainwright Evans[1] in these four paragraphs:

> Yesterday I watched a honey-bee die among the flowers — her wings frayed and ragged from long use, her body old, her vital forces completely spent. I had been watching her for some time when she abruptly stopped her work on a dandelion near my doorstep. For a full minute she groomed

[1] "Mother of a Million" in *Better Homes & Gardens* 1933.

herself carefully. Then suddenly she dropped from the blossom. — She could not fly.

After a few vain efforts to use her wings she began a frantic march back in the direction of the hives, about 200 feet away. Minute after minute she toiled prodigiously through that interminable jungle — the clipped grass of my lawn, forcing her way through towering growths twenty times as tall as she. Never for an instant did she pause in her effort to bring home to the hive that last pitiful drop of nectar in her honey-stomach.

But the effort was too much for her. Unable to hold the pace, she fell on her side and lay quiet. I thought it was all over. Then suddenly she went into violent action again. Now she seemed to have given up all thought of getting back to the hive with her load of nectar. Instead she began a kind of dance, very similar to those curious nectar and pollen dances which returning field-bees often perform on the combs to attract the attention of the other bees when they have found some new source of nectar or pollen.

She coursed in circles, in a small clear space amid the grass. Gradually the circles grew smaller; she worked in toward the center and at last sank down again. Her queer little dance of death had ended. When I finally picked her up she lay quite still. And it seemed as if I heard from somewhere that last, abruptly falling, fading note which ends Grieg's "Butterfly". . . Only this was no butterfly. . . I have no wish to sentimentalize over the incident; but there seemed to be a wild beauty in it, and nothing tragic. — She had simply worked herself to death. . ."

Nothing tragic in it! — Mr. Evans, it *was* tragedy! And, it would seem, a symbol of the very apotheosis of patriotism. One-for-all.

Just why is it that on certain days bees collect mainly nectar from flowers to "digest" into honey; on others specialize on pollen gathering, to get food enough for the larva brood; and on yet others seek and bring back quantities of propolis, a sticky glue from bud-coverings, a sort of patching plaster for the hive? These products are imported at the right time, in the right order and in almost exactly the right amounts. Supposedly. How are these specifications arrived at? How many allotted to the job? By whom? When? Who cancels the orders, if changes of temperature, man's interference, or other hive conditions, make cancellations sometimes necessary? Who manages the bee colony? — Of course, no one. No one individual. Though we speak of the "queen" (whom the ancients called the "king," before discovering he was an egg-layer), far from being a ruler, she is indeed the steadiest worked slave in the group and obeys her attendants' directions. Hers is a monotonous mechanical labor if ever there was one; though maybe not *hard* work; going on day after day; laying, laying, laying, up to five thousand eggs a day; eating what she is fed only; never once leaving the dark prison of the hive after she begins that routine. Never does she resent the directions of her guards; eats from their mouths; has but one choice ever as to depositing those eggs. Yet that one choice is a vital one, involving a veritable black magic: she can *at will* (?) lay a fertilized or an unfertilized egg! In her wonderful large shining body she preserves in separate compartments her own ova and the sperm-cells given her by the drone at her one mating. If she elects to lay a virgin ovum, untouched by a sperm-cell, that ovum will develop into a drone bee, a male! Such eggs she will deposit only in oversize wax chambers which the comb-builders sparingly provide for that purpose. All other eggs, she permits to be fertilized as they escape, and all will eventually become either queens or workers female in form yet immature to the end of their days. In this respect, she has mastered perfect birth-control, even though 5000 eggs per day does

[237]

not suggest much control in other respects. — A drone, then, is always fatherless, but always has had a grandfather, the one on the maternal side.

The queen does not lay queen-eggs. There are no queen-eggs. The supernaturally canny workers raise their own queens by over-feeding — or better to say, by better feeding. When they see — or foresee — that for good and sufficient reasons a few young queens ought to appear on the scene, they construct special bulging wax-cells as big as the end of a man's little-finger. Into each they *transfer* an ordinary egg from an ordinary cell, gorge its larva with a particular food from their crops; keep its mother away, that she may not murder her daughter — a possible successor! — and lo, in the fullness of time appears a large, sexed queen, made to order. These sexless workers *know enough* to do that! Further, they know, and without spinster jealousy concede that this young sister must have drones to choose from, and so allow her a nuptial-flight outside. Something has made them see that *for themselves*, for the good of the colony, sex equipment is a detriment, a hindrance. And so they control the love affairs and economics of the hive to the end that from fifty- to a hundred-thousand sterile spinster workers are born to match one mother and a few-score males! Efficiency. Yet almost antithetical to a Nazi order. . . Moreover from the day of their birth these spinsters know how to feed and care for babies of their own class as if they themselves were mothers. And they never allow a queen-daughter to meet a queen-mother — for that would end in murder. — Now, how, without "a whisper from God," do they attain all this wisdom! No wonder that a bee-keeper named Maeterlinck could say after a lifetime among his hives: "Of all the inhabitants of this globe, bees and ants possess the highest degree of intellect after that of man." He seemed dutifully impelled

to put in that last phrase and to use the word "intellect";
yet both these notions are today very much in question.
Several modern scientists would leave out the clause and
substitute "instinct" for "intellect" — and then go on to as
much as confess: "Well, what difference does that make!"
We are no nearer the bees.

Prescience. Clairvoyance. Instinct. Words, Horatio!
Reflect a moment: Worker bees whose life in Summer is
so short (lasting from three to 6 weeks, depending mainly
on how much work is got out of their wings) that they have
never experienced a Winter, or if they have will not endure
even to the next Summer; act *as if* they realized that the
colony's preservation over the ensuing Winter depended
absolutely upon their storing up good supplies for it —
honey which they themselves will not live to eat. Notice
their treatment of drones: magically aware that drones are
a necessary evil, it, the Spirit of the Hive, sets about to
create a few. The large drone-cells, in each of which the
queen will lay one drone-egg, have first to be constructed;
a few dozen here and there among the vast array of normal
brood-cells. — If this be not intention, what is it? — Though
only three or four drones can hope to succeed finally as
consort to the several young queens of the hive — and to
die as a result — scores stay around through the Summer.
They are allowed to eat at will from the public honey stores,
without adding a mite in return, and would go on being
parasites all Winter. But no, with the first frosts comes a
slaughter of the innocents. Practically all drones, useless
now, are killed or driven forth to starve; they who in Spring-
time were so cared for! This inexorable law of the hive is
applied even to sister-workers who endeavor to carry-on
with maimed bodies or tattered wings. If such do not
ostracize themselves, as usually they do — they are ruthless-
ly mob-murdered or dragged out and left to die. To this

perfect communist community the State is everything, the
individual but an incident.

What executive Thing determines how many bees shall
start constructing new honeycomb cells; determines when
it is wise to start? To call it Spirit-of-the-Hive is obviously
but to make an oral noise. There are some fourteen separate
occupations in a hive from week to week and squads of
workers must perform them at the right time. Which workers are to be detailed? To which occupation? How are the
bees appointed who meanwhile "police" the hive of dirt and
debris, dead bodies and invading insects? How is the squad
selected which will act as ventilators; partly to keep currents of outer air stirring on hot days, partly to evaporate
the watery fresh honey to a proper, "ripe" consistency? . .

In many ways bees are not mere creatures of habit, any
more than you and I. Rutted and routined in some things
(even as you or I), they definitely lay plans and they seem
to meet new situations. It is certainly baffling that creatures
whose lives are so strongly dependent on a "homing instinct," should decide and determine to leave the old home
for a new. To swarm. And once established there, immediately lose all interest in coming back to where they were
born. Swarming is no sudden wild rush for the goldfields.
Whatever the particular cause behind it on a given occasion, it is prepared for with the thoroughness of an army's
general staff. They go forth boldly, never because "times
are hard," never in a "period of depression." Exactly the
contrary. Leaving prosperity behind them, and good fields
of bloom, they risk danger, pioneer hardship, perhaps entire
destruction, in order to face poverty again. It is the perfect
Social Revolution. The dead hand of old age and authority
seems their greatest peril as a race.

Some three weeks are required for a queen to develop
from egg to mating-flight; the young queen is the one to

"lead" a swarming and establish a new colony; therefore plans looking like conscious plans must be laid fully that long ahead. Scouts must go about for days seeking out suitable places. To whom they report; upon whom lies final selection, who can guess? The day dawns for which they — but only half the colony — are waiting. Those who intend departing equip themselves with supplies of honey, wax, pollen, propolis from the old home, to be food and furniture for the new where regular work may be for a time in chaos. — Yet, should the day set turn suddenly cold or a rain begin, the emigration is usually postponed, even for several days.

Last May I witnessed a swarming from one of my hives, which impressed me as to this plastic adaptability — not a priori to be expected in robots. Just after sun-up I noted that something unusual was afoot — or a-wing — at one point in the line. I saw that it was a "hive Sunday, the only Sunday known to bees," their swarming holiday. Hundreds of bees were rushing from the overcrowded hive; they became presently a nebulous sphere of milling bees twenty feet in diameter. The hum thereof was the swarming-hum; it could have been heard and recognized from at least a hundred yards away. They were "possessed," as the ancients used to say about hysterical patients. They vibrated, and did not fly away. . . . Not wishing to lose even 10,000 out of my two million slaves, I greedily assembled the parts of an empty hive. Hardly had I fitted it together when I saw an oval ball of bees begin to form around a hickory branch near by. — The young queen must be up there. Before very long she might be off to the woods. How strangely they acted, that slowly swelling golden-brown oval with its nebula of circling satellites! Not at all the colony I knew yesterday. Not at all like the dutiful and unaffected majority left in the home below, who were

NOW THAT WE HAVE TO WALK

carrying on business as usual because a Voice had bid them stay. . . . Above them, precisely as the Old Master Maeterlinck has written, an age-old marvel was being re-enacted:

> "It is the triumph of the *race*, the victory of the future: the one day of joy, of forgetfulness and folly. . . the solitary day upon which all eat their fill, and revel to heart's content. It is as though they were prisoners to whom freedom at last has been given. . . .They come and go aimlessly — they whose every movement has always had its precise and useful purpose. . . On this day man can approach them, can divide the glittering curtain they form as they fly round and round in songful circles; he can take them in his hand. . . they will submit to everything and injure no one; today they are bewitched."

Inside the lump on the hickory branch, smothered yet not suffocated, was the queen; she who presently will be mother of millions. Slowly parting the quivering, animated jelly, I searched within it until I found her. — One needs no second look; her inch is every inch a queen. How un-honeybee-like she looks! Monarch of the commonplace, for fertility is the cheapest commodity on earth. She is an obvious *symbol* of fertility. Whereas a man's fecundity is only potential and adventitious, such that *one* can be father of every United States inhabitant; she can and will be mother to every member of her clan — until death does its part! . . .

I took her gently in my fingers knowing she would not sting, for hers is a weapon never used but against royalty — and who was I to claim that standing! (— Even a robot bee, female but neuter, can sting but once, and that act is suicide.) Putting her within a little wire "suds-maker" (which serves as a cage temporarily) which was at once covered by hypnotized swarmers, this I slipped beneath the brood-frames of the new hive. . . In an hour some third

[*242*]

of the bees had entered; but on the hickory limb the majority remained. An experiment occurred to me: to sprinkle these outside with water. I used a whisk broom; they "thought" it was raining, perhaps. After a few moments of huddling together closer, they began whirling into the air and returning to the hive — but not to the new hive, as I naturally expected. But back to the old hive they went! They had abandoned their queen. Also they had shifted their purpose when faced by shifting weather conditions. . . . But of course, they would soon try swarming again; their old home was too crowded. And they did, a week later. . . .

Information passes through a colony like smoke. Quicker than the population of the globe heard of the Pearl Harbor treachery, every daughter-bee learns of the death of her queen; or of other news: of the location of an unguarded hive to be pillaged; of a store of accessible honey uncovered in a workroom, etc. — A few Summers ago I was lunching on the lawn, a saucer of honey and one of raspberries on the table. A foraging bee finally found the honey. I marked her with a smear of raspberry juice. She returned in some two minutes. Presently another arrived. As fast as they came I marked them. So fast they came that I fell behind. Now the honey was covered with numbers crowding in. — Yet, before that first-comer discovered it the honey had sat there well over half an hour.

By what means is communication between individuals accomplished? By antennae touching solely? By wing-sounds? In their hummings is a whole language: menace, distress, contentment. They perform (as one poet puts it) "an ode to the queen," "the song of abundance," "psalms of grief," and "a war-cry of the fight." Their antennae are made up of 6,000 platelets! — do they "hear" through some of them? — as well as smell? Or are their "ears" tympanums

upon a leg-joint, like the ears of crickets and grasshoppers?
Critical opinions differ. . . Professor Leuenberger, a famous
Swiss expert, in 1930 laid the efficacy of the bee telegraph
to smell; asserting that scent is *detected* by the antennae,
but *emitted* by a tiny yellow gland on the lower abdomen,
the scent of whose secretion is different in each colony, and,
he guesses, is varied somewhat at will to transmit different
emotional messages. . . Possibly there are several types of
communicating, and that all the senses are employed. —
Even as with us. A bee should understand any kind of
sign-language since it has five eyes; on two of which are
thousands of separate facets — in order to take in images
from virtually every angle.

A queen, it is said, can lay her own weight in eggs in one
day. That is rather "busy" to start with; yet that adjective
has not been applied to bees for centuries without further
reason. For instance, while 10,000 workers *could* (as a matter of strength) carry in a pound of nectar from flowers, it
usually requires twice that many. As four pounds of nectar
are turned ("ripened") into one pound of honey, about
80,000 bee-trips are necessary — to over a million blossoms —
just to produce the honey as honey. Yet 80,000 *more bees*
in a colony have to keep going the many other hive industries: secrete wax, make and cap cells, store pollen,
guard the entrance, feed young, evaporate ("ripen") that
pound, et cetera. Mathematically, then, 160,000 bee-days
are about what is required to fashion a pound of honey.
Then calculate what it means in bee-miles, bee-hours, bee-
lives for one colony (of say, 50,000 inhabitants) to wind
up a season with 500 pounds which is a good average Summer crop! To assist in this algebraic feat, remember that
it has been established that one and one-half miles is about
the usual roundtrip length of each working flight.

Away from the hive bees unless accidentally pressed or

caught, will not sting. It is for hive protection only that
the sting functions, not for an individual's safety. Every
bee-keeper knows his own measure of susceptibility to
being stung. Some people can scarcely approach a hive
without danger; others apparently do as they please with
bees. Is it a human body-scent which makes the difference?
Or one's unhurried, unafraid motions? Veteran opinion
inclines to the latter. Yet, some old-timers tell me they
think a secret state-of-fear causes an odor to come from the
sweat glands which bees — and dogs — detect; and this
scent goads them to aggression. — Well, since we have to
concede so much to psychic phenomena in discussing bees,
we might as well allow this conjecture, too. As for myself,
my infrequent stings vary widely in severity. A pang of
quick agonizing pain, a day or two with moderate swelling, and the stab is forgotten. However, once a single
thrust delivered at the base of the throat, and once a prick
under the arm-pit, places where lymphatic glands or ducts
seemed to be hit, or were close by, intensified my heartbeat
almost to suffocation in less than sixty seconds. Too dizzy
to stand, I lay flat on my back for an hour, the terrific effect
transcending my knowledge of physiology. . . .

"A swarm of bees in May is worth a load of hay;
A swarm of bees in June is worth a silver spoon;
A swarm throughout July is hardly worth a pie."

Yes, and a swarm of bees on paper, not as much as a
cloud of vapor! If you are irreverent towards bees and their
magic lives, get a glass-lined observation hive hooded by
removable shutters — and watch! Possibly you approach
it to scoff; but you will remain — to pray. For breeding
humbleness in cocky friends, it is wonderful. If you are
skeptical as to what superior food will do for children, or

as to the potency resident in a hormone or a vitamin, watch a huge-sized queen, tenfold longer-lived, produced by absolutely nothing but special feeding for *five* days. If you are loath to accept "spiritual" explanations in the affairs of bees, see for yourself that without hesitation, without fear, a sexless bee will leap to defend its fellows with a sting — and becomes a social sacrifice. If you imagine you could ascribe bee-havior merely to set-and-patterned tropisms, raise these "creatures of habit and instinct" for a year or two — and you will discover that every fact I have mentioned here is contradicted; every generalization stated suffers many an exception.

Probably men will never get that grasp and control of their social problems and governmental mechanisms that the bees have attained. The reason it is said that bee-haviour in government and in personal relations is "perfect," is that, given the colony as is, and given the ecology of the bee as is, the two fit hand-in-glove. Both colony and its ecology are practically unchanging from year to year; over inconceivable aeons of time the insect and its ways have altered little. The bee's government and social relations are biologically, physically, *evolved* out of its direct contact with and manipulation of environment. In its "decision" at a given instant, there is no theory, no alternative involved; no new "problems" arise, except, statistically speaking, once in a very great while. If accidentally they do arise, the particular bees involved ignore them, in the main, though they perish by them. They act in our eyes as if they were "at complete loss" at times; they "act stupid." But the mere fact of the bees' ancient origin, proves how little and how seldom such new local dangers arise. — Not often enough to be worth trying to adjust to. Evolution of its body has come from the insect's bodily and functional contact; its sense organs, mouth parts, antennae, wings, all and each are a perfect fit into one ecology. . . . Man's line has steadily — since the lemurs — been moving away from *fitting* into any one environment, social or ecological. —Which is the reason for so much present social bungling. His work in his world is infinitely diverse; as are his relations with his fellows. He has evolved practically no specific biological machinery to cope with either environment; what is evolved is highly generalized.

Man's brain is the ideal substitute — in theory — for the specific evolutionary equipment of the bee. Yet it must always deal in brain-ways, in intellectual ways: by logic, syllogisms, classificational generalities. And, alas, the acts and emotional functionings of most men are simply not to be managed, maneuvered, changed, or even understood, in that fashion. Very seldom does the rank and file say just what they mean or mean just what they say; most animal organisms do. Because they have to. And cannot help it. Human affairs, matters of everyday living together must be worked out through (and manipulated by) a sort of abstruse differential calculus, a handling of divers variables; whereas the mill run of reformers and radicals are apt to consider such matters as problems of arithmetic — or at best, of an algebra in one or two integral unknowns. Yet, in hive economy, where at any one moment in a May day, at least five major variables must be gauged and grappled with, we have to recognize a calculus mind, a slide-rule mastery, that should humble any mechanical engineer or efficiency expert.

It is unlikely that men in future will evolve at all in directions better fitting the mechanical age. Century by century, the more man knows of physical science, the less that knowledge continues coming *through the senses;* from contact and experience, since most of that knowledge is very modern, teleologically speaking, and is today largely expanding. But this "knowledge" is not coming so much through the sensorium as through extensions of the sense organs. Through sense-tools like the microscope, fluoroscope, thermacouple, electric eye, X-ray, and the like. Man has no muscle-knowledge of what an atom weighs, or a ton. Nor can he *see* an angstrom unit of light. Therefore, evolution toward adaptation, if it comes at all, can work only in the mysterious brain cells, because the organism *man* is not biologically affected in the process of gaining adaptation in such "vicarious" ways. Perhaps man will never even know how to create or manipulate a revolution without cruelty, force and killing. Yet revolution is what has kept bees forever young.

The tools I have spoken of above do not influence the neural, physiologic or germinal biology of man's body. Hence they will not function as "acquired characteristics" or function at all *hereditarily*. The opposite has been true of insects. To take but one amazing glimpse of that fact, consider the wax-cell.

Its cross-section is hexagonal, its inner angles 120°. Why not cylinders? Because the walls of cylinders have not the *bracing* qualities of a prism. Six-sided prisms fit into one another, the walls of one slightly bracing the walls of all the others contiguous. The walls being thin as tissue-paper, need bracing. . . The angle at which the pyramidal ends of the cells take off from the sides, proves to be the angle at which human physicists calculate would permit the cell (and therefore comb), to be constructed with the very minimum amount of wax! Since no animal-form is hexagonal in section, a larval bee, or an adult bee gulping honey into it, would not exactly fit a hexagonal prism; yet the first and governing consideration was strength, the second, minimum of material, both for walls and for ends of the queer cell. — Looks like careful figuring, doesn't it?

HUMILITY BEFORE BEES

But the best other answer to the puzzle is to say: the strain of bees which first hit upon or approximated hexagonality, tended to survive better than the strains which did not. Hence heredity finally preserved that form and that strain. —Yet, I admit I do not exactly know what "approximating hexagonality" really means. (But I am going to go on thinking about it.)

＊　　＊　　＊

Ask a man, "Just what is the YOU in you?"—"Why, the ego, the soul.". . . "Then are *you* who stand talking there but a disembodied spirit?" He ruefully shakes his head: "Of course not." "What then?" "It must be my brain.". . . "What part of your brain?" "The thinking part.". . . In spite of the obvious objections you now raise by pointing out that an utter idiot lives a long life; so do all animals which do not think — at least, in the way we do; that lonely, ex- cised human and animal tissues are being kept alive and growing — and have been over two decades — in bottles at an experimental laboratory in New York City; he still feels bound to say that he is an ego, a unique person. If a bee could be asked about its ego, it could reply only, "I am everywhere and nowhere; I am a spirit doomed for a certain term — to fly the day — and no man can point and say: it is I!"

> What is the ultimate answer, and if there be
> An answer, how is it finally given?
> This the eternal enigma, the lifelong question
> Paraded before the mute and irreconcilable hills.
> We are apportioned miracles, nothing more,
> Sprung from the loins of the ledge.
> We are given to see
> The prodigal wild apple living in beauty,
> Never to reach fruition, never a reason.

[249]

NOW THAT WE HAVE TO WALK

We are shown the intolerable awe of the midnight sky
When the snow squeaks and the mind reeling with light
Is drawn down astral lanes to its certain disaster.

The answerer is hidden infinitely, the questioner
Puts his old riddle with slitted eyes, thin lips.
Slowly the echo dies down corridored years. The inquirer
Is bonded to dungeon walls where the gray old rats
Abound, the metered moisture drips,
And the darkness crowds.

—Louis Stoddard

❖   ❖   ❖

Winter Cordwood

Dawn after dawn as I look to the woods
above the hill pasture gold-lit by sunrise,
an insistent urging descends,
an apparent beckoning of twigged fingers: "Come up,"
the Winter-numbed woodlot whispers in its naked sleep,
"I am waiting. Come cut, thin out,
purge me of my gnarled and evil parts
and leave me upright, sound, ready for Spring,
ready for life once more, for growth.
—I too would not grow old.

Surgeon of Nature, with your tools, your skill,
you save me serving yourself and your loved ones.
Wood warms you twice, to cut and to burn.
Your presence here warms me into living;
the sound of axe and saw wakens me.
Here the rewards of poetry await you:
in all my trunks the suns of June
to feel against your cheeks; in stove and fireplace
the croon, the subtle hiss of Summer
—my magic madrigal. . . Come."

HUMILITY BEFORE BEES

Oh, to be hale myself, renewed and ready for Spring!
To wield the knife of action; to defy cold;
to compete with strong men again;
to control the plunge and wallow of horses,
inhaling the acid smell of their sweat and mine;
to feel the sting of helve within my palms,
the bite of blade, the swishing stroke of crosscut,
satisfying bone and sinew and the lust for achievement,
loosing cramped muscles, freeing encysted minds;
—*to warm all my world with maple and oak!*

❋   ❋   ❋

BIBLIOGRAPHIC

Here I turn you over to the specialist and the expert: to librarians and booksellers; to the local museum. It is their business to know (or to know how to find out) what books are good books in any line of science, in any sort of hobby.

As for walking and its allied pursuits, if one does not know where to go roundabout, or what groups are organized for promoting tramps and trails; some one of these sources probably can help you:

Local Museum of Natural History
Boy Scout organization
Girl Scout and Campfire Girls
National (or local) Association of Audubon Societies
Appalachian Trail Conference (see Ch. X)
State Conservation or Recreation authority
American Nature Association, Washington, D. C.
Bear Mt. Trailside Museums, Bear Mountain, N. Y.

Of course there are a number of appropriate periodicals; four of the best of these covering a generalized field are: *Nature Magazine,* 1214 Sixteenth St., Washington, D. C.; *Natural History Magazine,* Am. Mus. of Natural History, N. Y. City; *Audubon Magazine,* Nat'l Ass'n. of Aud. Societies, 1006 Fifth Av., N. Y. City; *Frontiers,* Phila. Academy of National Science, Philadelphia (5 times a year).

Many publications emanate from State Museums, State Departments of Conservation, or their Fish and Game authorities; U. S. Department of the Interior: its Park Service and its Forest Service; the federal Smithsonian Institution, Washington, D. C.; State Agricultural Departments (also Cornell University's Rural School and Farm leaflets); quite a number of state- and federal-aided universities and colleges throughout the country.

The majority of books on hobbies and natural history carry

extended bibliographies at the back covering recommended books along their line of interest. I know of two books which are themselves bibliographies. *Key To The Out-Of-Doors* by Hurley (as compiler), published by H. W. Wilson Co., manages fairly complete coverage of all books of this sort up to and partly including 1938. And a later attempt at the same end, published by the same house and compiled by Altsheler, 1941, is useful also. Its title is *Natural History Index-Guide*, indexing 3365 books and periodicals.

—And yet — the author would not be an author did he not at times contradict himself. At the outset of this section I said that readers were to be left to the librarians and booksellers; and now I am going to set down a small list, a very small list of some good book-buys whose fields are located in the territory covered by the present volume:

Title	*Author*	*Publisher*	*Year*
A Lot of Insects	Lutz	Putnam	1941
Nature Photography	Morris	Appleton	1938
Nature Guiding	Vinal	Comstock	1926
			(still good)
Nature Recreation	"	McGraw-Hill	1940
Country Living	Wilson	Stephen Daye	1938
Byways To Adventure	Teale	Dodd, Mead	1942
Grass-root Jungles	"	"	1937
The Golden Throng (bees)	"	"	1941
Pet Book	Comstock	Comstock	(4th Ed.)
Handbook of Nature Study	"	"	(24th Ed.)
Book of Wild Pets	Moore	Putnam	1937
Camping and Woodcraft	Kephart	Macmillan	1941 rev.
Of Ants and Men	Haskins	Prentice-Hall	1939
Instinct and Intelligence	Hingston		
Wild Flowers	House	Macmillan	1936
Indiancraft	Hunt	Bruce, Milwaukee	1942
Indian and Camp Handicraft	"	"	1938

BIBLIOGRAPHIC

Bird Flight	Aymar	Dodd, Mead	1935
Science of Life[1] (4 vols)	Wells, Huxley, Wells	Doubleday	1931
Deserts on the March[2]	Sears	Un. Okla. Pr.	1936
N. Y. Walk Book	Torrey et al	Dodd, Mead	1934
Down To Earth	Devoe	Coward-McCann	1940
Our Amazing Earth	Fenton	Doubleday	
Animal Treasure	Sanderson	Viking	
Our Mobile Earth	Daly	Scribner	
This Puzzling Planet	Brewster	Bobbs-Merrill	

"Natural History Hobbies for Human Defense" by Brammer, in Misc. pubs. #3, Cincinnati Museum of Natural History.

"School Museums, Field Trips, Travel . . . Objective Education," N. Y. State Museum Bull. April, 1942.

The Nature Almanac — Am. Nature Ass'n. 1930 (reference book on nature ed.)

✿   ✿   ✿

The Nature Field Book series, about 24 titles, published by Putnam.

The Nature Library, about 12 titles published by Doubleday, Doran.

✿   ✿   ✿

On the general subject of outdoor life and the mystery and charm of nature, a very great deal of enjoyment and information will be found in reading almost any book by the following authors:

---

[1] A college course in Biological Sciences.
[2] One of the notable books of the decade.

BIBLIOGRAPHIC

L. H. Bailey

E. H. Baynes

William Beebe

John Burroughs

Frank M. Chapman

Alan Devoe

Raymond Ditmars

Walter P. Eaton

Jean Henri Fabre

E. H. Forbush

"Grey Owl"

R. W. G. Hingston

W. T. Hornaday

W. H. Hudson

Ernest Ingersoll

Sir James Jeans

H. K. Job

Wm. J. Long

Olive T. Miller

E. A. Mills

John Muir

T. Gilbert Pearson

D. C. Peattie

C. G. D. Roberts

Theo. Roosevelt

Archibald Rutledge

H. R. Sass

Sam'l Scoville

E. T. Seton

D. L. Sharp

Alex. Sprunt jr.

Henry Thoreau

Bradford Torrey

W. M. Wheeler

Henry Williamson

Mabel O. Wright